The Coding Dojo Handbook

a practical guide to creating a space where good programmers can become great programmers

Emily Bache

The Coding Dojo Handbook

a practical guide to creating a space where good programmers can become great programmers

Emily Bache

This book is for sale at
http://www.lulu.com/shop/emily-bache/the-coding-dojo-handbook/paperback/product-21273101.html

This version was published on 2013-10-29

ISBN 978-91-981180-3-2

This book was originally created using LeanPub (http://leanpub.com).

Contents

Foreword

Do you remember this old joke? A young man is on the subway, carrying a guitar case. He's a member of a band that is performing a concert at Carnegie Hall; and he's running late. He dashes off the train and up the stairs, and realizes he's lost. He knows that the performance hall is close, but he doesn't know the direction. So he stops an old man on the street and asks: "Excuse me sir, but how do I get to Carnegie Hall?" The old man looks at the lad with his guitar case and says: "Practice son, Practice."

It is a fundamental truth that all professionals practice. Of course professional musicians practice; and so do professional athletes. Lawyers practice – they rehearse testimony and closing statements. Doctors practice, on cadavers, dummies, and even suturing oranges. All professionals practice.

What do we, programmers, do to practice? We write code of course. Lots of code. We write code at work, and then many of us go home and write more code. We do this because we love writing code; it is a passion for us.

But not all forms of practice are equal. Some ways to practice are better than others. Professional athletes practice games, but they also practice drills. Musicians practice their performances, but they also practice scales and etudes. These other forms of practice are designed to emphasize, and therefore improve, certain skills – especially those skills that are hard to acquire and easy to lose.

That's what this book is all about – a special way to practice that emphasizes certain skills that are hard for programmers to acquire and easy for them to lose. Those skills include working together as a team, the disciplines of Test Driven Development and Refactoring, good design skills, and many others.

In this book Emily Bache describes one of the most popular activities to come out of the Software Craftsmanship movement; an activity that is sweeping across our industry: The Coding Dojo. Based on a martial arts theme, the Coding Dojo is a meeting in which enthusiastic software developers, intent on self improvement, engage in purposeful practice for the purpose of refining their skills.

The Dojo gives a formal structure to such practice. That structure is complete with rituals, disciplines, rules, and procedures that promote effective learning and minimize distraction. The Dojo is a safe place to practice with, and learn from, others. Best of all, the Dojo is *fun*!

In this book you'll get a feel for just how much fun this can be; because Emily avidly describes the fun *she* has had in setting up, running, and participating in Dojos. Her enthusiasm is contagious. You'll read about her adventures, successes, failures, and just the overall great time she's had while learning, and helping others to learn, in the Dojo setting.

With her lively and readable style, Emily teaches us how to set up a Dojo, and what the principles, rules, and procedures are. She tell us how to deal with what she calls: "Dojo Disasters"; and she describes the various forms of practice such as Kata and Randori. And, perhaps most importantly, she provides a catalog of the exercises that she has found most beneficial in a Dojo.

But there's more to this book than a description of Dojos. While describing the disciplines and principles of Dojos, Emily also engages us with a very cogent and enlightening description of some of the most important software disciplines of the last decade. These include Test Driven Development, Refactoring, Continuous Integration, Test Automation, and many, many others.

In short, while this book is a wonderful workbook for practice; it is also a tutorial in *what* to practice. The subtitle says it all: This book is about making good programmers great.

Is that your goal? Do you want to be a great programmer? Then you don't want to miss this book. Because to become great, there's only one absolute rule: Practice child... practice.

Robert C. Martin

17th November 2012

Introduction

As a professional programmer, how do you learn new skills like Test Driven Development? Pair Programming? Design principles? Do you work on a team where not everyone is enthusiastic about good design and writing automated tests? How can you promote good practices amongst your colleagues?

I've worked as a programmer for many years, and these kinds of questions have come up again and again. This handbook is a collection of concrete ideas for how you can get started with a coding dojo where you (and your team) can focus on improving your practical coding skills. In my experience, it's a fun and rewarding activity for any bunch of coders.

Learning new skills inevitably takes time and involves making mistakes. In your daily work environment where the focus is on delivering working production code, it can be hard to justify experimenting with new techniques or to persuade others to try them. When I attended my first "Coding Dojo" with Laurent Bossavit and Emmanuel Gaillot in 2005, I could see these kinds of meetings could be a fun way to effect change.

When you step into the coding dojo, you leave your daily coding environment, with all the associated complexities and problems, and enter a safe environment where you can try stuff out, make mistakes and learn with others. It's a breathing space where the focus is not on delivering solutions, but rather on being aware of what you actually do when you produce code, and how to improve that process. The benefits multiply if you can arrange to bring your whole team with you into the dojo. Through discussion and practicing on exercises, you can make a lasting impact on the way you work together.

Following the dojo I attended in 2005, I brought Laurent to my (then) workplace to show us all how it was done, and from there I began to facilitate coding dojos in various other settings. I've done them with my immediate colleagues, user groups, at conferences, and more recently as a paid consultant brought in to do training with teams. Inspired by Corey Haines, I've also led "Code Retreat" days, which is a kind of scaled up coding dojo. All these events have been good fun - coders enjoy coding! We've had excellent discussions, learnt from each other, and written a significant amount of clean code and tests. It seems to me that acquiring skills like TDD, Refactoring and pair programming is a long process - it takes years - and it is a lot more fun and rewarding if you can get a like minded group of people to join you on that journey.

This handbook is a collection of practical advice drawn from my experience, with concrete ideas for how you can get started with your own coding dojo. There is a catalogue of "Kata" coding exercises that you can try, and advice about how to choose one for your particular situation. There are many useful resources on the internet which you can use to augment your dojo, and some are reviewed here.

Kent Beck once said *"I'm not a great programmer, I'm just a good programmer with great habits"*[1]. What are you doing to improve *your* coding habits? This is the book with the advice and encouragement you need: get together with some like-minded people and hold a coding dojo! It's fun!

---

[1]page 97 of "Refactoring" by Martin Fowler

Acknowledgments

This book has its origins in the work of Dave Thomas, who introduced the idea of the Code Kata, and Laurent Bossavit who came up with the idea of the Coding Dojo, and co-founded the first one in Paris. Over the years many others have also contributed to develop the idea and the practice. I'm especially grateful to Laurent Bossavit, Emmanuel Gaillot and Fredrik Wendt, pioneers who I have collaborated with and learnt from in the dojo.

Over the years I have met many people in coding dojos, and I am grateful to have learnt so much from them. There are some I have met in the dojo who I count myself particularly lucky to have learnt from and with. I'd like to mention especially Marcus Ahnve, Johannes Brodwall, Enrique Comba Riepenhausen, Andrew Dalke, Greg Dziemidowicz, Dave Hoover, Jon Jagger, Arnulf Krokeide, Robert C. Martin, Dave Nicolette, Thomas Nilsson, Danilo Sato, Christophe Thibaut, Francisco Trindade. Thankyou to all of you.

Some of the material in this book is drawn from the codingdojo.org wiki[2], which is owned by Emmanuel Gaillot. I was one of the many early contributors there, and I am very grateful to everyone who participated in forming that wiki into a useful resource.

Many of the Katas in this book have been designed by other people, and some of the other material as well. I'd like to

---

[2]http://codingdojo.org

thank everyone who gave me permission to include their Katas in the catalogue, their Dojo Disasters, their wisdom born of experience: Johannes Brodwall, Emmanuel Gaillot, Terry Hughes, Jon Jagger, Robert C. Martin, Roy Osherove, Matt Wynne.

I also want to thank Corey Haines for the work he has done popularizing the Code Retreat, which although different in form, has a philosophy in congruence with the Coding Dojo.

I must also thank my children's violin teachers, especially Marika Wirung and Sven Sjögren. They patiently demonstrate good pedagogy week after week, using the Suzuki method. I have learnt a huge amount about how to teach, by observing them.

I would like to thank all the people who reviewed this book, including Johannes Brodwall, Olivier Demeijer, Nicolas Dermine, Greg Dziemidowicz, Jonas Granqvist, Yves Hannoulle, Jon Jagger, Arnulf Krokeide, Mark Longair, David Read, Anders Schau Knatten, Martin Svalin, Joel Trottier-Hebert, Fredrik Wendt, Joseph Yao. It's a much better book because of your comments.

How to Read This Book

This is supposed to be a practical, useful manual. Dip in and out, or read it all the way through, as you wish. The first section is all about the various coding games and activities you can play with. If you're experienced running Coding Dojos already, you might want to skip most of the second section, which is largely about how to set up and run a new dojo. The third section explains some of the skills you're trying to improve at, and gives you help choosing the right kinds of exercises for your Deliberate Practice. The fourth section, the Kata Catalogue, lists all the Katas I've found useful in the dojo, and you can choose one to tackle at your next meeting. You will be holding a Coding Dojo, right? That's part of the deal with buying this book!

Dojo Disasters

Most of the time we have a really good time in the dojo, and people come away feeling positive about the experience, and what they learnt. Occasionally though, things don't work out so well. In several places dotted about the text you'll find "Dojo Disasters" - little stories where I, and other dojo pioneers, have learnt the hard way.

What is a Coding Dojo?

A Coding Dojo is a meeting where a bunch of coders get together, code, learn, and have fun. It's got to be a winning formula! Programmers generally love the plain activity of writing code, away from managers and deadlines and production bugs. When they've got over their shyness, most are delighted to show others how well they can actually write code, as well as to pick up tips and advice from them. Throw in a suitably puzzling Code Kata and a safe environment to discuss topics like design, testing, refactoring, choice of code editor, tools... and you're away! You'll hardly be able to stop them talking and writing code and learning from one another!

There are few obligatory elements to a coding dojo, designed to promote the aims of learning and having fun. Within those constraints, you still have a lot of freedom to adapt the form and activities according to what you discover suits your group, or in other words, makes it more fun. Some people just prefer to meet with some like minded coders and hack at something together. That's absolutely fine, and can be great fun, but I think you'll learn more if you add just a little more structure.

Essential Dojo Elements

For a dojo I think you need to:

- Hold an intro and retrospective

- Write tests as well as code
- Show your working
- Have moderation or facilitation

The intro and moderation are designed to make sure everyone feels safe to experiment and learn. The retrospective makes sure you reflect on what you've learnt. Writing some tests as well as code sets you up with a feedback mechanism on whether your code is working as you expect. Demonstrating how you write the code, not just the code you end up with, means you learn a mechanism to produce good code, not just what good code looks like. Those elements - intro, retrospective, moderation, showing working, and tests - are what sets a coding dojo apart from any other kind of coding meeting.

The rest of this book explains how a Coding Dojo works in detail.

Section 1: Collaborative Games for Programmers

There are many ways to organize a group of programmers so that they can code and learn together, and in this section I'd like to introduce some of them. There are *whole-group-programming-together* activities, *working-in-pairs* activities, and *look-at-me-coding!* presentations. I like to talk about "collaborative games" for programmers, because that's what we're doing. There are rules, there are activities, there are people talking and helping each other and learning.

What is a Collaborative Game?

A Collaborative Game is one where there is no individual winner, but rather all the participants must contribute to a solution, and you together beat the game itself. I'm a pretty big fan of board games, my cupboard at home is overflowing with strategy games like *Settlers of Catan, Seven Wonders, Ticket to Ride, Dominion, Diplomacy...*

None of those titles are a Collaborative Game - in all of them you're competing with the other players, although there is often a degree of collaboration too. Recently I've been discovering I actually quite enjoy playing purely collaborative games, too. For example, *Forbidden Island*, where it's a race against time and tide. The players must work together to gather all the treasures and fly off in a helicopter before the island sinks under the sea. Apart from anything else, when I play it with my children, no individual has to lose, and that makes for fewer tantrums!

I think the coding part of a Dojo should be like a collaborative game, you're not out to appoint a winner, you're there to collaborate and contribute, and solve something together.

Randori

Coding in a group is fun, and this activity takes it to the extreme. Everyone can see the code, projected onto the wall, and everyone gets to write some code, taking it in turns to type. When you get a bunch of half a dozen coders working on the same problem like this, you'll quickly find there are at least a dozen opinions on what code to write! There are some rules designed to keep the Randori on track, and give everyone the best chance to contribute, teach and learn. It can be high volume, intense coding.

A Randori requires almost no preparation, since no-one need have done the kata before. You have to come to design decisions through discussion, and by explaining everything so clearly that whoever has the keyboard can understand what's going on, and decide what direction to take. When you get your turn at the keyboard, suddenly you're in the spotlight, it's hard to think straight, and you have a limited time. You have to choose carefully what code you write - this is your chance to decide exactly what code goes into the codebase, don't waste it!

Before you start, have someone setup their machine, connected to a projector, with an empty failing test. There are a few different variations on exactly where to put the computer, see the next section "Randori Variants". You'll also need to agree who should be the starting pair, and a Pair Switching Strategy.

If the person with the keyboard has an idea for the first test to write, you could just let the pair get started coding. At some point though, you'll probably want to step back and do some analysis of the problem on a whiteboard. (See the chapter on "States and Moves of TDD", the "Overview" state).

The whole group needs to understand the code that's being written, since everyone will have a turn at the keyboard. Some things are better explained with a sketch on a whiteboard, than by dictating a list of keystrokes to the driver.

In turn, the pair at the keyboard must explain what is going on, so everyone can follow. The audience should give advice and suggest refactorings primarily when all the tests pass. At other times the pair at the keyboard may ask not to be interrupted. See the Randori Rules:

Randori Rules

1. if you have the keyboard, you get to decide what to type
2. if you have the keyboard and you don't know what to type, ask for help
3. if you are asked for help, kindly respond to the best of your ability
4. if you are not asked, but you see an opportunity for improvement or learning, choose an appropriate moment to mention it. This may involve waiting until the next time all the tests pass (for design improvement suggestions) or until the retrospective.

You could appoint a meeting facilitator, who has a special responsibility to see that these rules are followed, but that might not be needed for an experienced group who are familiar with them. (See also the chapter Facilitating a Dojo Meeting)

Dojo Disaster: Code Ridicule

This dojo disaster story is by Matt Wynne

It was 2008, and I was at an international software conference. I'd only started going to conferences that year, and was feeling as intimidated as I was inspired by the depth of experience in the people I was meeting. It seemed like everyone there had written a book, their own mocking framework, or both.

I found myself in a session on refactoring legacy code. The session used a format that was new to me, and to most of the people in the room: a coding dojo.

Our objective, I think, was to take some very ugly, coupled code, add tests to it, and then refactor it into a better design. We had a room full of experts in TDD, refactoring, and code design. What could possibly go wrong?

One thing I learned in that session is the importance of the "no heckling on red" rule. I watched as Experienced Agile Consultant after Experienced Agile Consultant cracked under the pressure of criticism from the baying crowd. With so many egos in the room, everyone had an opinion about the right way to approach the problem, and nobody was shy of sharing his opinion. It was chaos!

We got almost nowhere. As each pair switched, the code

lurched back and forth between different ideas for the

direction it should take. When my turn came around, I

tried to shut out the noise from the room, control my

quivering fingers, and focus on what my pair was saying. We worked in small steps, inching towards a goal that was being ridiculed by the crowd as we worked.

The experience taught me how much coding dojo is about collaboration. The rules about when to critique code and when to stay quiet help to keep a coding dojo fun and satisfying, but they teach you bigger lessons about working with each other day to day.

When to choose a Randori form, and what to work on

The Randori approach is most suitable for groups of about 4-10 people. Above that the discussions can get out of hand, and each individual doesn't get much time at the keyboard.

If you choose a Kata that is too difficult, it can be frustrating for the group to get nowhere near finishing it using the Randori form. Particularly at first, try to pick a really simple kata so you can get a sense of achievement from completing it, and having time to make the code really clean.

Pair Switching Strategies

Timebox

- Each pair has a small (5 or 7 minutes) timebox.
- At the end of the timebox, the driver goes back to the audience, the copilot becomes driver and one of the audience step up to be copilot.
- Use a kitchen timer or mobile phone that beeps when time is up.

Note: anecdotally, you need a longer timebox when working in a statically typed language than a dynamically typed one: you have more text to type! Try 7 minutes for Java or C++, 5 minutes for Python or Ruby.

This switching strategy makes it more likely that everyone has a go at driving. The main disadvantage is that you get cut off in the middle of what you're doing, and it can be harder for the next person to pick up where you left off.

Dojo Disaster: Refused Bequest

Kind of like in the Liskov Substitution Principle, if you inherit something you have no use for, it's a sign something is wrong. In the particular dojo I'm thinking of, we had a diverse group where some people had been coding with TDD for many years, and others were young and inexperienced - still at university. We were doing a

Randori in Pairs, switching pairs every 10 minutes. With

only three or four pairs, we got round the table several

times. About half way through the kata I went back to a particular machine, and realized I hadn't seen this code before. No, really, it was completely new! The code I had written half an hour previously to pass the current failing test was gone. Vamoosh.

It turns out that one of the less experienced programmers didn't understand my code, so he deleted it. In fact he didn't understand any of the code, and had deleted it all and started again from scratch!

Has that ever happened to you, only with production code? It certainly has to me. We had a great retrospective that time, discussing code readability and reuse.

Ping Pong

1. The driver writes the first test and then hands the keyboard to the copilot
2. The new driver makes the test pass
3. They refactor together, passing the keyboard as necessary.
4. The original driver (who wrote the test) sits down in the audience, and a new person steps up, initially as co-pilot.
5. As step 1, with the new driver (the person who made the last test pass)

This ensures that you don't get broken off in the middle of a sentence like you do with Timebox, and that each person writes both a test and some production code. It has the disadvantage that the pair can spend so long perfecting their code and tests, that not everyone gets a turn at coding. This is particularly likely if there are people present who are unfamiliar with TDD. When they get the keyboard they might not know what to write, and spend a long time before they understand the help they're offered.

NTests

The pair at the keyboard write and implement N tests, where N is usually 1, 2 or 3. Then a different pair steps up to the keyboard. Alternatively only half of the pair is switched after N tests.

I suspect this one only works with pretty experienced TDDers, since you have to be skilled at writing really small tests, and building the solution up gradually. For some coders, this format could tempt them to write too large granularity tests so they can retain the keyboard for longer.

Randori Variants

Driver/Navigator

I've seen it happen many times that an otherwise competent programmer sits down at the keyboard in a Randori and suddenly has no idea what to type. The stress of being in the spotlight causes some kind of biochemical reaction that makes your hands seize up, your mind go blank and your armpits sweat profusely! In this case it can help to separate concerns so the driver is no longer expected to think, only type. Rather like in rally-car racing where the driver drives, and the navigator sits in the passenger seat and tells him or her in detail where to go.

In the Randori, have the non-keyboard wielding half of the pair become the Navigator. This means they do all the thinking, and simply instruct the Driver what code to write. The Navigator can be really specific, even down to the level of "ok, now type 'filter open bracket lambda space x colon...'". Of course most of the time the Driver is actually feeling fairly relaxed, since they only have one thing to worry about: telling the computer what to do. The Navigator can probably just say "filter the list with a lambda expression...". Dictating a sequence of keystrokes is something of a last resort, for when the Driver is having a real rabbit-in-headlights moment!

Once the Driver has been guided by the Navigator for a while, hopefully they'll feel they understand what's going on. When it's time to switch pairs, it could be good to put them into the Navigator role next, and pick a new Driver from the audience.

Co-Pilot stands up

If you're finding the group is not easily able to follow what
the pair with the keyboard is up to, you might find it helpful
to have the co-pilot, (or navigator), stand up while the driver
sits down. This will force them to talk louder. The co-pilot
could also stand closer to the projector and point to things on
the big screen as they talk. (The driver needs to sit facing the
screen in this case, so they can see what's being pointed at).

Facing away from the group

This can be useful if the pair at the front is constantly
interrupted, and the discussions often get out of hand. Put a
separate table at the front so the coding pair can sit facing
away from the group, towards the projector. Without eye
contact with the group they will hopefully find it easier to
concentrate. It can also be less scary since it's easier to ignore
the "audience". It can make it easier for the pair to get going
and actually write some code without being pulled in ten
different directions by all the backseat drivers.

The main danger with this is of course that the group can
get sidetracked and stop paying attention to the code being
written.

Randori In Pairs

Split into pairs (or trios) and work on a Kata for 45-90 minutes.
It can be good to have a facilitator, (who has done the kata
before), who spends the session going between pairs, helping
them. The facilitator can give feedback on the code and tests
as its being produced, and spread knowledge.

In the dojo, one of the principles says we show our working, not just the code we end up with. In this case you are showing your working to your pairing partner, but you need some way to share what you've learnt with the group. There are a few variants:

- after coding, plug each computer in turn into the projector, and have each pair explain how they wrote it.
- Some or all pairs perform the kata for the group (perhaps at a subsequent session). See Prepared Kata
- switch the pairs around and repeat the kata from scratch - if you do this several times over the course of a day, then the learning and new approaches get spread around the group. (This is the approach at a Code Retreat).

This is a good alternative if the group is getting a bit large for an ordinary Randori, ie with more than about 10 people.

Musical Chairs Programming

As with a Randori in pairs, except every 10 minutes, ring a bell and have one half of each pair get up and go to a different computer. Try to arrange it so you get to pair with lots of different people, not just have everyone move one space to the left and end up pairing with the same people all the time.

As a variant, have an option so people can choose not to code in some sessions. These non-coders stand in the middle and discuss the problem, then can choose to go back to coding the next time bell rings. This can enable knowledge to spread through the group faster.

Usually you'll have all the pairs working on the same kata in the same programming language - there will still be a wide variety of approaches!

I've also done this with everyone doing the same kata, but in several programming languages. It works well so long as a critical mass of people know each language in use.

Dojo Disaster: It's all Greek to me

One time I was at a conference, and we decided to do a Randori in Pairs, switching pairs every 10 minutes. Each pair got to set up their own environment, and choose a programming language. Of course at the time Ruby was the next hot thing, and although almost everyone there was a Java programmer, half the pairs chose Ruby, or even something more sexy, like Clojure or Erlang. As we circulated around, it became clear that hardly anyone knew what they were doing in these languages, and there was much hacking, googling and tearing of hair. It was actually pretty boring, unless you happened to be pairing with one of the few polyglot gurus!

Following that conference, and similar experiences, Jon Jagger actually changed the way you set up a new Cyber-Dojo session so that all participants have to use the same programming language.

Prepared Kata

You can learn a lot by watching an expert at work. You can learn a lot when teaching. In a prepared Kata demonstration, someone has practiced the kata many times, and is showing the group their best solution. Not just the finished code, but the entire process from empty editor via Test Driven Development to a full working solution. As they code, they should explain their reasoning and choices, so everyone can follow what is happening and why the code turns out like it does.

The person at the keyboard is setting themselves up in a particularly vulnerable position, and it takes quite a bit of courage. It's not easy to code in front of an audience and talk at the same time. You will usually choose a pairing partner from the audience to support you. This person has a particular responsibility to point out omissions, typos etc, but actually everyone in the room should try to be supportive and kind. Comments and suggestions for improvements can be experienced as distracting though, so you're free to ask people to save them for the retrospective.

If you are new to kata performance, it can be less stressful to prepare together with a pairing partner. You can learn a lot from your pair during practice sessions. When it comes to the performance, you'll be able to demonstrate good pair programming in action as well as TDD.

If you're in the audience watching a Prepared Kata performance, your first priority is to make sure you understand what's happening. The idea is that you follow in enough detail that you'll be able to go home and reproduce the whole Kata for yourself afterwards, or in the next dojo meeting. The pair at the front should always be willing to stop and explain their thinking. Your other job is to try to think of better ways to do the Kata. Did the pair produce a good design in the end? Are they taking small steps, especially when refactoring? Would a different order of tests lead to better design insights?

You should set a time limit for the performance, to be sure there is enough time for the retrospective. At the retrospective, everyone should give feedback and constructive criticism. Both the performers and the audience should have learnt something. The ultimate aim is that everyone should be able to go away and do the Kata again, and do it better!

Screencasts

Some notable software practitioners have made screencast recordings of themselves performing Prepared Katas, and put them out on the internet. You could spend many hours watching people do different Katas with various programming languages, tools, and TDD approaches. I feel a little torn about the usefulness of doing this. One of the main attractions of the Coding Dojo for me is that you actually get to meet people, and that the learning is two-way. In a screencast, the presenter is not learning directly from me as a viewer, which is very different from the situation in a Coding Dojo. It's also not possible to ask the presenter to pause and explain their reasoning, or discuss an alternative approach with them.

I know it's not always practical to get people physically together in a dojo to discuss coding techniques though, so watching a screencast may be the next best thing. It also shows the value of having a number of standard Kata exercises out there, which many different coding dojos use. If I already know the Kata being performed, and have practiced in a particular programming language or style, it can be a real eye-opener to see someone else do it differently.

I'd much rather invite someone into my dojo to do their performance though. That would be a lot more fun than watching them on a screen! I guess this is why I like going to software conferences so much. There's often some kind of dojo or hands-on coding session where you can learn new techniques.

Code Retreat

Code Retreat is a day-long practice-intensive event for programmers, popularized by Corey Haines. There is a lot of information about it on his website[3]. Taking part is intense, and should really stretch your coding ability. Corey has also set up an annual "Global Day of Code Retreat", where thousands of programmers take part in hundreds of Code Retreat events around the world. It's a pretty impressive global phenomenon! I do recommend the buzz you get taking part in a day when thousands of people are tweeting about improving their programming skills, and you can virtually "hang out" with other coders in far off countries.

The motivation and aims of a Code Retreat are basically the same as with a coding dojo - you're all there to improve your coding skills and have fun. In fact, a Code Retreat fulfills the Essential Dojo Elements! The main differences with a normal coding dojo are basically that it's all day, you always code in pairs, and you repeatedly tackle the same Kata - traditionally Game of Life.

Structure of the Code Retreat Day

- Gather together early, typically 8:30 am
- Facilitator introduces the day, overall aims and format.

---

[3]http://coderetreat.org

- 1st coding session, learn about the problem, no additional rules.
- 2nd coding session, use TDD & clean code.
- 3rd coding session, focus on simple design & clean code, maybe introduce a constraint.
- lunch, 90 minutes, hot food.
- 4th coding session, introduce a constraint.
- 5th coding session, introduce another constraint, or just try to code your best solution.
- closing circle & retrospective, typically end 5pm

Some groups fit six coding sessions into a day, but that's pretty tiring!

A coding session comprises:

- 5 minute intro, presenting the challenge for the session.
- 45 minutes of coding in pairs.
- 5 minutes retrospective.
- 5 minute break.

So each session lasts about one hour. At the end of each session you delete all the code you wrote, and you start from scratch again in the next one, with a new pairing partner. The idea of deleting the code is to make it less stressful - you're not there to deliver anything, the only tangible outcome is learning. It also means you can try out new approaches without the baggage of previous code slowing you down, and your new pairing partner doesn't have to spend ages reading the code that's already there.

You switch pairs every session so you get a chance to learn with and from a wide variety of people, using different approaches, programming languages and tools.

Game of Life Kata

The problem you work on is the "Game of Life" Kata. This is a fascinating kata with a large scope and many possible solutions. The idea is that by repeating the same Kata all day, you get to concentrate on learning coding skills, not delivering a working product. You quickly get to know the kata well enough that you can stop worrying about how to produce a solution, freeing your mind to reflect on the way you're coding.

In the first session, you can drop the requirement to write tests, and just hack around understanding how a solution could look. Work out a datastructure for representing an infinite (!) grid, for storing cells or cell states. Sketch on paper some example positions where each rule comes into play, causing survivals, deaths and births. Work out if you can visualize the position using ASCII art or some simple html graphics.

In the later sessions, you should know the kata well enough to start stretching yourself. The facilitator introduces challenges and constraints like "Really Small Methods" or "mute pairing", which are described in more detail in the next section "Playing with Constraints".

The Game of Life Kata is actually too big to comfortably solve in any one 45 minute session, even after a fair amount of practice. Some people extend the last session in order to give people time to "finish" it, but this can be counterproductive. Most people fail at it, and those who don't could miss out on one of the charms of the Code Retreat day - that you're left wanting more!

Practicalities

You generally do a Code Retreat on a Saturday, on your free time, so everyone is pretty motivated to be there and wants to learn. Some people hold them internally at companies on work time too.

It is generally more fun with more people to switch pairs with, so you should invite at least 10 people to the event. The facilitator gets round each pair less frequently as the number of them increases, so probably set an upper limit around 40 people.

A Code Retreat should be free to attend, so you need to get a sponsor. The sponsor should provide the venue, tea and coffee throughout the day, and a hot lunch. Some sponsors also give participants free stuff, prizes in a lottery, and a glass of wine or beer at the end of the day. It's good to relax together a little while after a hard day's coding and learning.

Code Retreat Variants

The Code Retreat format has been used many times, and is quite prescribed. For your first Code Retreat, I recommend you follow the advice on coderetreat.org[4] closely. Once you've done that, use what you've learnt in the retrospectives, (and in your coding dojos!) to make improvements. Several people have already been designing variants, and publishing information about how to run them.

J.B. Rainsberger has set up a "Legacy Code Retreat" event, very similar in form to a normal Code Retreat, but using the "Trivia" problem. The Game of Life Kata doesn't necessarily

---

[4]http://coderetreat.org

stretch your skills with refactoring, but this one really does! I haven't been to a Legacy Code Retreat, but as I understand it, you spend all day working on this code, honing your refactoring skills, and learning about techniques such as Approval Testing.

That's just one that I know of that has been reasonably successful. I think there is plenty of scope for designing other whole-day Code Retreat variants. There are many skills to learn and many Katas that continue to give new insights with repeated practice.

Playing with Constraints[5]

Once you've got to know a kata, you no longer need to spend all your mental effort on just finding a solution. You can concentrate on a host of other aspects of *how* you code, and try to improve them. The idea of these games is to force you out of your comfort zone, and give you no choice but to work on a particular coding skill. For example *how* you design, or do TDD, or pair, or use your tools.

These are games you can play when doing a Randori or Prepared Kata forms, although they're commonly used with Randori in Pairs. As with the Kata catalogue, this list is not exhaustive! These are games I've enjoyed, and I've listed them roughly in order of difficulty.

Make a test list

You're not allowed to write any code for the first 10 minutes of the coding session. You must write a list of test cases on paper, and decide the order you plan to implement them in. Then when you code, cross off the test cases as you implement them, and add new test cases as they occur to you.

Forcing yourself to write a test list on paper can help you understand the roadmap and goal of your coding session. It

---

[5]Many of these games were originally published on http://coderetreat.org

can iron out misunderstandings with your pairing partner, and avoid big refactorings later.

Keyboard only

Do you know your editor well enough to get by with only the keyboard? Try unplugging your mouse and disabling your trackpad! Once you get used to it, it's actually a much faster way to work. As programmers, it's good for us to be really proficient with our tools.

It's been said that typing is not the bottleneck - that coding is actually a cerebral activity, and writing it down is the easy part. While this is true, once you've decided on a design, being able to get it into your editor and up and running quickly shortens the feedback loop.

Use a plain text editor

Do you know your programming language well enough to work without your IDE? Can you produce working code without the benefit of syntax highlighting, auto-complete, and inline compiler errors?

This game forces you to understand how your programming language actually works, and makes you think hard about what you're actually doing. Instead of a plain text editor, you could use the tool Cyber-Dojo, which has a similar effect.

Really small methods

No methods in your codebase (including tests!) may be more than n lines long. Any time you have a method with more than n lines, you must perform "extract method" and make it smaller. For a language like Java or C++, which are quite verbose, n = 4 is quite challenging enough. For a language like Python or Ruby, n = 2 is a realistic goal.

This game helps you focus on the fourth rule of Simple Design[6].

No conditionals

Can you write code with strictly no "if" statements? Of course, you can! You just have to use higher-level constructs like polymorphism and object composition instead. Ban keywords like "if", "unless", "?" (the ternary operator), and see what it does to your design.

No loops

Can you write code with strictly no loops? Of course you can! You just have to use higher-level constructs like "map", "filter" and "reduce", or just use recursion. Ban keywords like "while", "for" and "foreach" and see what it does to your design.

Mute Pairing with Find the Loophole

You have to pair program without speaking! One person writes the tests, the other implements the code. The person

---

[6]http://c2.com/xp/XpSimplicityRules.html

implementing should do the simplest thing that could possibly work, and make the test pass, before handing the keyboard back. They should take this to the extreme and actively look for ways to fake the result, or "find the loophole" that will make the test pass with little or no effort. Only if the fake is actually more difficult to write than a general solution should you actually implement something. The person writing the tests is forced to be really specific about what they want, and write communicative tests.

Note on refactoring: generally the person doing the tests refactors the test code, and the person doing the implementation refactors the production code.

I usually add a rule that if you think the test you've been given is too big or difficult to make pass, you can comment it out, write a better test, then hand the keyboard back. In this way you swap roles.

This game can help you to understand how tests become documentation. The design and requirements as far as possible should be in the code, not just in your heads.

Note: this game is quite difficult for people new to TDD, they have enough trouble defining any tests at all, without the constraint of not being able to talk! In that case, you could allow talking, but still have one person define all the tests, and the other write the production code.

Collective Green Deadline

If you have a group working in pairs, you can use this constraint game to get people collaborating between pairs. In the middle of the dojo coding session, make an announcement:

all the pairs must work towards having all the tests passing simultaneously in 5 minutes time! You could say something like "The customer is coming for a demo!" or "There is a trade show we need to be ready for!" People should collaborate to get the whole group ready at the same time.

This game can help you understand the value of working incrementally in small steps and having a working system at all times.

Tools for the Dojo

You can hold a dojo quite happily using only your normal programming tools. An editor, a testing framework, maybe an interactive programming environment or an IDE. That's fine and might be all you need - you are after all trying to learn skills that will help you in your normal job, so working with your normal tools will be useful for that!

The tools I'd like to highlight here are specifically designed to help you to learn to improve the *way* you write code, and are useful in a coding dojo. First I'd like to go through some tool features that I've found useful in the dojo.

Test Run Logging

While you're in the middle of doing TDD, it can be hard to pay attention to how well your TDD session is going overall, so it can help to have a tool monitor your test runs. Every time you execute the tests, a tool can record the current time, and whether they passed or not. After you've finished working on a code kata, you can go back and review the data.

Logging test runs will show you how often you run the tests, and how large steps you're taking - generally small evenly sized steps is a good sign. The log can also help you discover if you're doing the TDD cycle well. A repeating pattern of failing tests followed by passing tests followed by several more passing test runs should emerge: cycles of Red - Green - Refactor. Some TDD failure modes become obvious.

If there is a long gap in test runs, followed by a passing run, it could mean you have taken a larger step and written a lot of code at once. Did you have tests for all that new code? Or maybe you were just spending a lot of time thinking, discussing, and designing?

If there is a gap between test runs, followed by one or more failing test runs, you might have been attempting a big refactoring and it didn't go so well. You might want to then practice the kata again, breaking the same refactoring into smaller steps with more frequent test runs.

A good tool for TDD cycle logging will also allow you to go back and see what code you had written between each test run, so you can check the reasons for gaps and sequences of failing test runs. It might also offer some automated analysis of how well you're doing TDD.

Revert to Last Green

If you're trying to improve your Refactoring skills, it can be useful to quickly and easily abandon a failed refactoring, and revert the code to the state it had at the last successful test run. You can attempt the same refactoring again, or do a different one. Any time the tests fail unexpectedly, you can evaluate if you want to revert the code to the last green run, and try again. That might be faster than working out the cause of the unexpected failure.

A good tool will let you easily see what's changed since the last passing test run, and let you quickly revert the code if you want to. If you have enough self-discipline, you can of course commit the code to a version control system every time the tests run green, but it's useful to have a tool to do that for you in case you forget.

Facilitator Overview

If you're facilitating a Randori In Pairs, you're constantly moving from pair to pair offering feedback and discussing progress. If all the pairs are using test run logging, a tool can help you to get an overview of everyone's current state. If you spot that a particular pair hasn't run the tests for ages, or if they've had a series of red test runs, you might prioritize going over to talk to them and see if you can help.

Even if you can't see all the pairs' status in real time, it does help to be able to see the test run log for a particular pair when you walk up to them. If the first thing you see is that the tests are red, they haven't been run for ages, and the pair appears to be refactoring, you'll have a more informed discussion with them.

Sharing code in the retrospective

If you've had several pairs working separately, in the retro-spective, you may want to view the final code each pair came up with. A tool can help you to view all the versions of the code from the same computer, and put them side-by-side on the screen.

Kata Starting Position Setup

When you come into the dojo, it's really annoying to have to waste time setting up your coding environment. You want to quickly get going practicing! Some katas have a small amount of starting code that needs to be set up in an editor or IDE. If you're practicing in an unfamiliar language or testing framework, you might need to install tools or download libraries.

Tool support can help with these problems, and by issuing a couple of commands you can get set up and ready to code in seconds.

Prepared Kata for online review

I've discussed before about Prepared Kata Screencasts and the pros and cons. If you want to make one, there are various tools available. I'd recommend finding a tool that lets the viewer scan through at a different rate to the speed you type when you record the kata. Viewers may want to skim past the easy boilerplate coding, and slow down when reviewing more complex parts. It can also be useful to see a diff that highlights which code has changed since the last test run, or since a previous test run.

Generally I'm not that interested in this kind of tool though - I'd rather get you into a dojo to do your prepared Kata with face-to-face real time feedback from peers. In my experience, it's much more fun and rewarding.

Kata catalogue

There are a lot of good code katas in the catalogue in this book, but there are loads more out there on the internet. A tool could help you find good ones for your situation, perhaps based on many people's reviews. Unsurprisingly, I'd be looking for a catalogue with detailed kata descriptions and advice, similar to what you'll find in this book.

Cyber-Dojo

This open-source tool was invented by Jon Jagger. He has a publicly available server at http://cyber-dojo.com[7] that you could use in your dojo. You can also find the source code for cyber-dojo on his github page[8], and instructions for how to set up your own server.

I've used this tool quite a lot in the dojos I've facilitated, and I do recommend it. It has all of the features mentioned above. It also enforces a constraint - you're coding in a plain text editor. That's not always a constraint I'm interested in enforcing, but the other features make it worthwhile. I haven't yet found any better tool to use in the dojo.

Coder's Dojo client

This is a free tool you can use for test run logging and visualization, available from the codersdojo.org website[9]. It's a ruby gem that you run on the command line, that can log test runs when you're working in pretty much any major programming language. It monitors changes to files on your filesystems, runs the tests and takes a copy every time you save the code. This means you can use your normal IDE or editor, unlike Cyber-Dojo.

I haven't been very successful using this tool in actual coding dojo meetings (see sidebar below), but I've found it pretty useful when I've been practicing a kata just by myself at home.

---

[7] http://cyber-dojo.com
[8] https://github.com/JonJagger/cyberdojo
[9] http://content.codersdojo.org/codersdojo_client/

It has a very nice visualization of your test run log, and lets you review your code step-by-step through the kata. It also has facilities for asking others to review your performance online.

Dojo Disaster: Tool Culture Clash

I was planning a refactoring kata, and I wanted people to be able to use their normal refactoring tools, but also review a test run log afterwards. I suggested that everyone installed the coder's dojo client. What I hadn't realized was that almost everyone was working on Windows, and had generally only ever coded Java. I was horrified to discover that installing a ruby gem then running a tool on the command line was completely beyond them!

I think if the tool had been a maven package or eclipse plugin things would have been different. Installing the tool was just taking too much time and distracting from the exercise, so we did the kata without test run logging on that occasion.

Other tools

There are other useful tools out there, including some commercial ones. I generally have much less experience using them, and haven't yet found any as good as the two mentioned above. Many of the features I've talked about could be easily added to other existing coding environments, and there are probably a host of useful tools we haven't even thought of yet. Given the readers of this book are programmers, and how much programmers love to invent tools, I'm sure my advice is going to become out of date rather rapidly!

Below are a couple of features of other tools that I know of, that I think could be useful to have in a dojo setting.

Constant Test Running

Some test runners will execute all the tests all the time, and with practically every keystroke you make, visually update the test status to red or green. This can help remind you which phase of the TDD cycle you're working in. It could help you avoid refactoring when there are failing tests, for example.

Tracking Code Smells

Some code smells can be automatically detected by static analysis, and a tool can track them. For example you might want to know if you've introduced a long method, or if you have managed to eliminate some deeply nested code. Your tool could produce a report of the code smells it found before and after you did a refactoring kata. Hopefully this would be an encouragingly short list by the end!

Of course, there are limits to how well a tool can review your code. You'll still want to show your code to your peers in the dojo and get human feedback.

Using Production code in the dojo

Normally all the code you work on in the dojo is toy code that you will throw away afterwards. Here I'll talk about situations where you might bring production code into the dojo.

When you know enough TDD that Katas seem easy

If you can do TDD well on code Katas then hopefully you'll be able to start doing it in your production code in everyday work. To smooth the transition, some teams like to hold dojos where they work on production code together. It can be so informal as that the team just pull the next story to work on from the task board, and take it into the Dojo. They follow the usual meeting format, including intro, discussion and retrospective, and work on the production code all together in Randori format. It can be a chance to get the whole team talking about real issues in the real codebase. You just have to be very careful to keep the atmosphere safe and constructive, keep doing TDD, and not disappear down any rabbit holes. (By that I mean continue to make progress in small steps, with tests, and not try to refactor the whole codebase in one go).

Mob Programming

Mob Programming is a whole-team approach to developing production code. The people who invented it call it "All the brilliant people, working on the same problem, at the same time, on the same computer". They also published a video "Mob Programming Time-Lapse Video - A Day of Mob Programming"[a] and explained more on their blog[b]. It seems to me to be similar to playing the collaborative programming game I call "Randori", but all day every day, to get work done. That could be fun!

[a]http://mobprogramming.org/mob-programming-time-lapse-video-a-day-of-mob-programming/

[b]http://mobprogramming.org

This Code is impossible to TDD!

Alternatively, you might be finding TDD really hard with a particular piece of legacy code. Get your most experienced developer to do some preparation, and practice TDD:ing a tricky piece of code. They can then show this as a prepared Kata to the rest of the team. The idea is to inspire everyone that TDD is possible after all.

Dojo Disaster: Not impossible, just too depressing

A consultant I know held a dojo for a team, and they were encouraged that they could do TDD reasonably well on the code katas he introduced them to. However, they complained that TDD was way too hard in their production code, because of the poor design of their system. The consultant was adamant that they could do TDD even in the badly designed code, so they challenged him to prove it. The consultant looked at their code, and spent a while scratching his head and poring over his copy of Michael Feathers' *Working Effectively with Legacy Code*. He came to the next dojo meeting with a prepared kata demonstrating TDD in their codebase, and showing some techniques for dependency breaking and isolating code for test. The team was suitably impressed, and were inspired to start using these techniques for themselves.

Another team at the company heard about this demonstration, and asked the consultant to come back and do the same for *their* production code. Again, he pored over his by now well-thumbed copy of *Working Effectively with Legacy Code* and then some additional hours scouring the documentation of some seriously powerful mocking tools.

When it came to the day for the dojo demonstration, the new team started out hopeful and expectant, looking forward to learning how to TDD in their codebase. Unfortunately things didn't go as well as the previous time. The consultant *was* able to get their code under test, but at a great cost. The team found all the convoluted isolation-breaking and mocking techniques far too scary and difficult. They eventually asked him to stop, it was so depressing seeing just how hard their code was to unit test!

Identify a suitable Kata from production code

Sometimes when you're working on production code, you find TDD working really well, and that the piece of code you're building feels small and self contained like a Kata. You might want to package it as such, and try it out at your next dojo. Others can get the benefit of practicing on a Kata where TDD works well, but yet is drawn from a "real" situation. Remember that for an exercise to work well as a Kata, it needs to be quite small and self contained, so that you can code it from scratch in 1-2 hours. There are a few Katas in the catalogue that arose this way.

Section 2: Organizing a Coding Dojo

In the first section we talked about collaborative games you can play while coding in the dojo. What a lot there are to choose from! This section has more practical advice for someone setting up and running a new Coding Dojo. I'll explain how you could structure your meetings, practical details to consider, and talk about the facilitator role. I'd also like to take the chance to explain some theory.

Dojo Theory

The basic premise is that in order to become expert at something, you need to practice. Raw talent, if such a thing exists at all, only gets you so far. Various theories of learning suggest that "Deliberate Practice" over a long period of time is at the heart of attaining expertise.

Deliberate Practice

"When most people practice, they focus on the things they already know how to do. Deliberate practice is different. It entails considerable, specific, and sustained efforts to do something you can't do well—or even at all. Research across domains shows that it is only by working at what you can't do that you turn into the expert you want to become."

– K. Anders Ericsson, Michael J. Prietula, and Edward T. Cokely, writing in the Harvard Business Review

So Deliberate Practice is not the same as reading code or even books about code, valuable as those activities are. As Ron Jeffries points out in his article "Practice: That's What We Do"[10], *"But what changes people is what they do, not what they read. How many diet books have I read? Am I thinner?..."*

---

[10]http://xprogramming.com/xpmag/jatPractice.htm

Deliberate Practice is not the same as experience gained while doing your job. It is when you actually seek out experiences that will stretch your skills just the right amount, and give you feedback that enables you to learn. I think that it takes a great deal of self-discipline to sit down by yourself and try to do a code Kata, and it can be difficult to get good quality feedback without someone else present or at least available to review your code afterwards.

Going to a Coding Dojo helps enormously because it's fun to socialise and meet other geeks, which means you actually do it, rather than always just intending to sit down of an evening and do a Code Kata instead of watching TV. At the meeting, when you're doing a code kata together, you challenge one another and you have to learn to accept criticism and defend your ideas. You get feedback on not just the code you produce, but your coding technique.

Mastering a skill like Test Driven Development takes a great deal of effort, and it's naive to think you can get all the practice you need while working on production code. Doing all your practice in the dojo is probably ambitious too. I think you'll need to put in some time on your own. If you've enjoyed working on a Kata in the dojo, you might decide you *do* want to switch off the TV for an evening and code it up again instead. You've become motivated by the thought that you can do even better than you did at the dojo, and are looking forward to the next meeting where you can show off what you've learnt.

The dojo should be a good place to meet skilled programmers, and maybe find ones you might like to work with in the future. Some companies sponsor public dojos as a place to recruit programmers for their teams, or to advertise the skills of their consultants. I see this as a happy side effect though. The real point of going to a dojo is to improve your skills, (and have fun doing so!).

Learning TDD and Downhill Skiing

One of the benefits of emigrating from the UK to Sweden as I have done, is the significant improvement in access to winter sports. I discovered I really enjoy cross-country skiing. It's much like hiking - trekking all day in beautiful terrain, hardly seeing anyone else. This winter, we were in the Norwegian mountains enjoying some cross-country skiing, and for the first time, I decided it might be fun to learn downhill skiing. Mostly so I could keep up with my children, who are keen skiers already! It's quite a different kind of sport - the skis themselves are very different, and of course the slopes are much steeper. While the children were at their ski school one day, I hired a set of skis and boots, and had a go.

The gentle beginner slopes were no problem, I could snowplough just the same as on my cross country skis. I knew this strategy wasn't going to get me far though. If I wanted to go on the steeper slopes and keep up with my daughters, I'd need to master more advanced, parallel turns. A snowplough involves having the skis in a V shape in front of you, and you widen the V on one side to turn in the other direction. For parallel turns, you have to get the skis next to each other, and swing your whole body from side to side as you swish down the slope. It's great fun once you can do it, but while you're learning it's pretty scary. For a fleeting moment while you're turning, both skis are pointing directly downhill, and you accelerate rapidly!

Still on the gentle beginner slope, I started trying to get my skis next to each other and alter my system of balance and orientation of my body with respect to the slope. It was chaos! Legs and poles and skis in all directions! A slope which I could previously do quite competently with a snowplough, was suddenly really challenging. On several occasions I was grateful for the safety catch that prevented my skis from sliding down the mountain without me.

After some more trial and error I began to get the feel for the new style of skiing, and with almost every run I was able to keep in control at faster speeds. Eventually I was able to tackle a much steeper slope than I would have contemplated on my cross-country skis.

So when you're sitting there doing a code kata using TDD and it feels really awkward, unfamiliar and slow, remember me flailing about on the beginner ski-slope. I know you can probably code a solution to the kata pretty quickly without any tests at all, just like I could ski down that slope with a snowplough. The trouble is, an approach without tests is unlikely to scale to bigger problems. Take some time, suffer some falls, keep writing those tests. With enough practice you'll eventually be coding like a TDD pro, swishing down the mountain with the wind in your hair!

Finding Or Founding A Coding Dojo

When I first experienced the coding dojo, it was such fun I looked around for ways to do it again! At the time there was only one dojo - in Paris - and since I didn't live anywhere near there, it was unfortunately not practical for me to attend. So my approach was to bring Laurent to Sweden to teach me how to do it. I figured that watching someone else doing something is a good way to learn to do it yourself. That probably applies as much to leading a dojo as any coding skills! It worked for me, anyway.

Look around for an existing dojo near where you are. Do some googling, check out meetup.com[11], talk to your friends. If someone has already founded a dojo, but is too busy to run a meeting right now, maybe your offer of help will be all it needs to get it off the ground again! In some cases though, you might find there has never been a coding dojo near where you live.

You might be able to get to a conference where one of the sessions will be a coding dojo. Have a look at conferences like one of the XP series[12] (in Europe), or a conference run by the Agile Alliance[13] (in the US). There might be an "XP Day" or a "Software Craftsmanship" conference, or a "Code Retreat" happening nearer where you are.

---

[11]http://meetup.com

[12]http://xp2013.org

[13]http://www.agilealliance.org/

If none of that works for you, founding your own dojo could be an excellent move anyway. Even if you've never been to one before, you know how to code, and how to have fun, right? You've also got this book to help you! As a first action, I'd recommend finding someone to co-found it with you. It's more fun that way, and just like with pair programming, you keep each other moving.

In one of the coming chapters I'll go through some of the practical questions you'll have to sort out when you're organizing your dojo. Before launching into that though, I'd like to tell you an encouraging story about a particular Coding Dojo. It's about how a group of enterprising Frenchmen got the whole thing started.

The original Coding Dojo in Paris

I talked with Emmanuel Gaillot and asked him about the dojo he helped set up in Paris in 2004, which he continues to be an active member of, eight years later. This is my retelling of what Emmanuel said. I started by asking him how he got started with the first coding dojo.

It was after Laurent Bossavit and I had both been at the XP2004 conference in Germany. We were intrigued by the idea of practicing coding with "Kata" exercises. Laurent floated the idea of meeting to practice these katas, and we joked that you could actually call it a "dojo".

At about that time I was also reading "Quality Software Management (volume 4)" by Gerald Weinberg, where he sets some challenges, including to "facilitate other people's change projects"[14]. I wanted to learn Ruby, so I asked Christophe

---

[14]Quality Software Management (volume 4) by Gerald Weinberg, page 94

Thibaut to be the catalyst for my learning, and to work on it as a change project with me.

Christophe, Laurent and I were all active members of the XP meetup in Paris, and it turned out there were several other people there who were interested in learning a language like Ruby. We also wanted to better understand the code-centric XP practices like TDD and simple design. So in November 2004 a group of about 6-10 of us met in a bar. We sketched a vision for a new kind of coding practice meeting, and it went on from there.

We were quite influenced by Open Space Technology[15] and very early decided that it was everyone's responsibility to direct the content of the meetings, and that we should always hold a retrospective. We also said that if we ever set a date for a dojo, and no-one shows up, then that is the end, no more dojos. We all have to take responsibility. So the first thing we do at every meeting is to set a date for the next one, and someone has to offer to host it or find a venue.

We started out by working in pairs all on the same kata, and it became a kind of competition to see which pair could finish first. It was fun. A couple of sessions we worked on the "Bowling Game" problem, and then I did some work on it by myself afterwards. At the next meeting I tried to explain what I'd done, but they didn't get it, so eventually someone suggested I should just code up the problem infront of the whole group.

That was really fun. I love theatre, I've done a lot of work as a director and stage designer. Giving a good Kata presentation turned out to be a lot like producing good theatre - the story of the code as it develops, the rhythm of the test cases, and the

---

[15]http://en.wikipedia.org/wiki/Open-space_technology

opportunity to inspire and move an audience. Performing a code kata was great because everyone had an opinion on what I'd written, and how they could have done it better. I realized how poor my skills really were - a real "humility" moment! It was really energizing seeing how passionate people were about coding, I realized I had to prepare more and get better at Ruby. My Ruby at the time looked just like Java!

The next week someone else wanted to show their solution, and the week after, and the week after that. For several weeks we did nothing but prepared performances of the Bowling Game kata! We were amazed at the variety of solutions and programming languages and design discussions. We felt it was really valuable to not just show the result, but to show coding techniques.

One meeting of course it happened that no-one had prepared anything, and we didn't know quite what to do. Someone suggested we stop, that it was the end of the dojo, but then we had been having so much fun, we didn't want to stop! So Laurent suggested that we work on a new problem, and each take a turn to show some code. Over several more meetings we refined the "Randori" format, with 5 minutes each at the keyboard.

It was at about this time that we held our first dojo outside Paris:

"The Coder's Dojo - A Different Way to Teach and Learn Programming"

presented by Laurent Bossavit and Emmanuel Gaillot at

XP2005, Sheffield, UK. *(This is the session abstract)*

If I want to learn Judo, I will enroll at the nearest dojo, and show up for one hour every week for the next two years, at the end of which I may opt for a more assiduous course of study to progress in the art. Years of further training might be rewarded with a black belt, which is merely the sign of ascent to a different stage of learning. No master ever stops learning. If I want to learn object programming... my employer will pack me off to a three-day Java course picked from this year's issue of a big training firm's catalog. Nuts to that - acquiring coding skills is not an "instant gratification" process. This workshop proposes to discover a way of teaching and learning programming in a more appropriate manner, respecting the depth and subtlety of the craft.

Presenting the workshop at XP2005 was a way for more people to share in our experiment. The idea was to show what we'd discovered, and maybe inspire others to start their own dojo. It seemed to be moderately successful at that. One person who was there had just introduced himself as "Bob", and it was only later I realized he was Robert C. Martin, the well known speaker and author. He blogged[16] about how he enjoyed the session, and that gave the dojo idea a real boost. After that, new dojos were started in Helsinki, Linköping, and several places in the US.

Our original dojo group in Paris split and multiplied too. There were new dojos concentrating on specific programming languages, or at particular companies (on work time), or only

---

[16]http://butunclebob.com/ArticleS.UncleBob.TheProgrammingDojo

doing Randori, or only prepared Katas... there was a lot of experimenting going on.

Laurent and I went to several more conferences talking about the dojo, but then in about 2008 we realized the dojo "meme" had spread quite far. We got some feedback on a conference session proposal that "everyone has a dojo these days, we don't need to learn more about it". I was surprised, I concluded that meant the coding dojo had become somewhat mainstream.

New people started coming to our dojo, I remember being impressed by Jonathan Perret who wasn't a consultant like the rest of us. He had worked on the same product for a long time, and said shocking things like "choices I made in this codebase 10 years ago still affect my work". He really emphasized writing whole programs, not just a class with an API. One time he blew us all away when he came and showed us the "Snake" game Kata in Ruby - complete and playable with a GUI - in an hour.

We are still meeting in the Paris dojo, almost every week, and we are still learning. We've been coding quite a few games recently - bat and ball, blokus, maze solving, Langton's Ant... as well as exploring other themes like RESTful api design, using monads, Quine programming... we have a lot of interests! Some of our members recently started a new coding event for children, based on the ideas of the dojo. Otherwise we're still doing Randori and Katas and using the meeting format we decided on all those years ago. It's all documented (in French) on our wiki[17]. I think we're having as much fun as ever.

My vision is that ultimately there will be a coding dojo in

---

[17]http://wiki.agile-france.org/cgi-bin/wiki.pl?DojoDeveloppement

every town and city. Going to it will become as normal for a coder as going to the gym, or training football.

What happens at a Coding Dojo?

Doing some planning in advance of your dojo meeting can help you sort out in your head what you expect to happen. It should also help you explain to people who you want to sign up for the meeting. When you make your plan, think about these elements, (you don't necessarily do them in this order):

- Introduce the Dojo
- Agree the activities for todays Dojo
- Code!
- Retrospective

There is a fuller description of each in the next section, with suggestions of how long to spend on each activity.

Introduce the Dojo

This doesn't have to be anything long or fancy, the purpose is to help everyone to feel safe, especially newcomers. If you've never coded in a group before, or you're new to the language and tools being used, it can be rather intimidating at first. You want to try to get everyone into a position where they're ready to take part in the dojo. Perhaps mention the Dojo Principles, go through the Randori Rules, or simply remind people to be respectful towards one another.

This part of the meeting could take from 2 - 15 minutes depending on how many newcomers there are and how much they want to know about the theory behind the coding dojo.

Agree the activities for todays Dojo

It's a good idea to get some consensus about what the group wants to focus on, and talk a little about what you intend to try to learn. If there is something you want to change compared with what happened at the last meeting, this is the time to mention it.

Again, this section of the meeting should be rather short, 2 - 10 minutes perhaps.

Code!

This is the main part of the meeting, (ie the most fun!). We're all coders after all, and we're here to improve our coding skills. Along with the coding, there should be plenty of discussion, questioning and helpful suggestions. The first section of this book is devoted to this part of the Coding Dojo - see "Collaborative Games for Programmers".

Retrospective

This is the part of the meeting where we reflect on what we have learnt in the Dojo. You could use any retrospective form or activity that you think would be helpful. For example you could ask each person to first write down something they learnt, something that surprised them and something they still don't understand, then go around each person asking them to share. The simplest way to do it is just a free discussion about what happened and what people thought about it.

You should be sure to reserve some time for the retrospective so it's not squeezed out by too much enthusiastic coding. Reflection is essential for learning. I suggest 5 - 15 minutes.

Practicalities

First book a date

My strategy when holding a new dojo meeting is to first fix a
date and time. Find one that suits the people you really want
to be there, and when you've decided on that, look around for
a venue. There's always someone who's got a spare conference
room, coffee area or games room[18] that you can borrow.

Meeting Length

If you have less than one hour it becomes difficult to write
enough code to learn something new, or have time to discuss
it. Two to three hours is my preference. It gives you time to try
out some ideas in code, and for everyone to contribute to the
discussions. If you have longer than that, you should break the
meeting up into different activities with a short retrospective
after each, as well as a longer retrospective at the end.

Some examples:

- The Paris Dojo meetings are around 2 hours in an
  evening, followed by socializing over a drink or two.

---

[18]If you can find a trendy startup to sponsor your meeting! (Not that I'm boasting or
anything).

- my local Python user group meetings are 3 hours in an evening, including first eating pizza and discussing Python news. The dojo part is usually about 2 hours.
- Code Retreats are whole day events usually starting at 8:30 am on a Saturday. There are 5 or 6 timeboxed 45 minute coding sessions, with a hot lunch in the middle of the day. (For more information see the chapter on Code Retreat)
- Greg Dziemidowicz runs dojos at his workplace (Nokia) that are 1 hour, using the code retreat format, except with only one 45 minute timeboxed coding session.
- When I go to a company to facilitate dojos with a team, I usually suggest 2 hour meetings.

Meeting frequency

How often should your dojo meet? Well of course the answer is - how often do you have the time and energy? These meetings should be fun to take part in, so you'll want to repeat your dojo. Repetition is essential to learning, too. Real life is likely to intervene and restrict the time you have available for them though. You could aim to meet weekly, biweekly or monthly, or just see these as one off events you hold occasionally.

Some examples:

- The Paris Dojo meets every week[19].
- My local Python user group meets monthly, and about half the meetings take a dojo form.

---

[19]except if the regular meeting night falls on Valentine's Day. They are romantic French people after all.

- In Stockholm we've held Code Retreat events two or three times a year.
- When I'm brought into a company to facilitate dojos with a team I usually suggest biweekly meetings.

Group Size

A coding dojo is no fun all by yourself, so you'll want to get some people to join you. I've never tried a purely virtual coding dojo, and I think an essential element is the rich interaction that happens when people are in the same room. I've had best results with about 5 - 15 people in a room together. Too small and it lacks variety of opinion and style. Too large and discussions become unmanageable and some people get left out. The optimum is probably about 8 people. Having said that, I've led successful code retreats with over 40 people present. You have to change some of the forms and practices, but in some way keep the purpose. If your group is large, consider splitting up into several dojos. See also the section on Code Retreat.

Some examples:

- The Paris Dojo is usually about 4-10 participants.
- My local Python user group is usually about 6-15 participants.
- When I'm brought into a company to facilitate dojos with a team I usually ask them to limit it to 15 people, and we start a second group if there are more teams interested in participating.
- Code Retreats I've facilitated have had 30-45 participants, and we split into two "closing circles" for the

retrospective at the end, with one of the ordinary
participants stepping in as a second facilitator.

- At conferences I've taken part in dojos with 20, 30, or
even over 40 people.

Physical layout of the meeting room

Exactly what you'll need will depend on the activities you've
chosen. As a starting point, assume you'll need a projector,
at least one computer with a coding environment set up on
it, a table to put it on, chairs, and a large whiteboard to aid
discussion. (A flipchart can work instead if you havn't got a
whiteboard).

For some activities, (for example a Randori or Prepared Kata),
you only need one computer for coding on, connected to a
projector. You want everyone to be able to see the the code,
the whiteboard, and to be able to discuss with the group. There
should be enough space for people to get up and move around,
point at the projected code and write on the whiteboard.

For other kinds of activities, (for example Randori in pairs,
or Cyber-Dojo), you might be working in pairs, and need
more tables and computers. You'll also probably want to
occasionally change the pairs who are coding. Often we'll
all sit around a large conference table, and when it's time to
swap, everyone gets up and moves to a different place around
the same table.

Which Editor or IDE?

Go for an editor and keyboard layout most people are comfortable with if you're going to be switching pairs during coding. Otherwise let each pair decide. If you're practicing a Refactoring Kata you may want people to have their usual refactoring tools available, which often means an IDE. Alternatively you could level the playing field completely by using a tool like Cyber-Dojo, where you edit code in a browser with minimal tooling.

If you're doing a dojo with an international bunch, there are going to be problems with the keyboard layout. Or even if you're not that international - sometimes you get people who use a Dvorak layout or have other such quirks. Quite frankly, some keyboards have their curly braces in the most stupid places, and as for quotation marks, underscores and colons, well, let's just say there's no consensus. Some countries, (I'm looking at you, France), even put the letters in different places!

Dojo Disaster: QWERTY trouble

Once I went to a dojo in Finland, where we were using a French keyboard, using Vi and programming Haskell. Let's just say typing *did* become the bottleneck!

Which Programming Language?

If your focus is on learning something else, like Test Driven Development, you'll want to choose a programming language most people in the group are already comfortable with. It helps you to focus on what you're really interested in learning. If on the other hand you want to learn a particular programming language, you could decide to learn it in the dojo. Take a Kata you already know well in another language, and solve it in the new language. It really helps to have at least one person present who knows the new language well though. Otherwise you spend half the time googling basic syntax and error messages.

Work time or Free time?

If you ask people to give up their free time in order to come to the dojo, you'll likely get a different kind of person coming. They'll often be motivated and enthusiastic about learning, and willing to spend more of their free time in preparation or individual practice. The downside is that the people who really need to learn new coding skills won't ever turn up.

If you can persuade your manager that a coding dojo is a good use of work time, then you might be able to bring your whole coding team into the dojo, even the more reluctant people. In the best case, it will be so fun and rewarding that the reluctant people will become enthusiastic :-)

Another context I've run dojos in is at conferences. It's a different dynamic - still work time - but more enthusiastic people, who usually don't know each other at all. It can be great fun, but as it's something of a one-off event, you don't learn anything very deeply.

Who should you invite?

Well, good programmers who want to become great programmers! Start by asking the kind of people you think you could learn something from to join you. Remember what the Dojo Principles say about mastery? Find people who can broaden your coding horizons. That's not to say that you shouldn't also find some people who want to learn the same things as you. Look at the section Teaching and Learning in the Dojo for ideas of what you could aim to learn together.

Dojo Disaster: Clam-up

A friend of mine, Fredrik Wendt, also facilitates company in-house dojo sessions. On one occasion he found the dojo wasn't working very well. No-one seemed to want to step up to the keyboard and code in front of the group. When he tried to spark a discussion about TDD he found few people willing to speak, and those that did ventured only uncontroversial opinions. Eventually Fredrik worked out the reason for this. One of the people in the dojo was the boss who decided the salaries of the rest of the group! Most people had totally clammed up in fear. When Fredrik went back for the next dojo with the same group, he insisted the boss stayed away. They had a very different, much more talkative and rewarding experience! So the advice is - tell the bosses they are welcome to the introduction, but should leave once the coding and discussion starts.

Colleagues or Acquaintances?

If you go to a dojo at a public user group, or a conference, you'll experience coding with some people you have hardly met. You get exposed to their neat tricks with the language and editor and see other ways to code. You might be able to code in a language or environment you're unfamiliar with, or pair program with people who are far more skilled than anyone you normally work with. It can be a rather intimidating experience though. And you might have to give up your free time to do it.

If you go to a dojo with people you already work with then you'll probably still learn some new neat tricks with the language and editor, and you might still get to try out a coding language and environment you're unfamiliar with. The real benefit of it though is that you can bring up issues and discussions that you never normally have time or energy for, and try to get a team consensus around them. Should we be writing the tests first? What are our coding standards? How do we want to use mocks?

You're working on toy code that no-one has a big personal stake in. You know it may be preserved in a repository branch somewhere but you're not still going to be maintaining it in 5 years time. It's a safe environment to bring up issues, discuss them, and hopefully change the way you work in your production code afterwards.

Facilitating A Dojo meeting

Okay, so you've booked a date, a room, some people have agreed to come and you're looking forward to your dojo meeting. How do you prepare? What do you do at the meeting to get it to run smoothly and to create a fun learning environment?

Preparation

Review the section earlier in the book about a typical Meeting Outline, and decide whether you plan to follow it. If you've decided on a particular Kata, print out some copies of the description that you can hand round at the meeting. Prepare some slides to help you present the dojo introduction, or a small stack of index cards with notes to speak from. Do enough that you feel confident to stand up and get the meeting off to a good start.

If you have already decided on the Kata you plan to do at the meeting, you might want to take a closer look at it. You don't have to do it all the way through, in fact, it might be better not to. You want to leave lots of room for people to find a new and better approach, not just get them to reproduce your pet solution. So do have a look for a good Kata, read the section in the Kata catalogue "Contexts to use this Kata", and perhaps start writing a bit of code that could turn into a solution to it. You want to do enough preparation that you'll be able to answer questions about why you're doing this problem, help people to get up and coding quickly, and have them set off in roughly the right direction. Then be prepared to learn with them!

During the meeting

It's when the coding starts that your job as facilitator gets interesting! Your job is to create a good atmosphere, prompt interesting discussions, and keep the code growing. This is going to need social skills, and programmers as a group don't have the best reputation for emotional intelligence, shall we say. I guess you know the joke about how to spot an extroverted programmer? They look at *the other person's shoes?!*

I don't think that's really fair, I've always found programming to require good social skills. As Martin Fowler once said "Any fool can write code that a computer can understand. Good programmers write code that humans can understand". Programmers also work in a team, mentor junior developers, discuss requirements with stakeholders, interview potential hires... Facilitating a dojo might stretch your existing skills, but it shouldn't be fundamentally new or out of your grasp. See it as an opportunity to improve your social skills as well as technical!

Once the coding starts, you should intervene to curtail un-helpful discussions, or to remind people of the dojo principles. You want to maintain a healthy atmosphere where people feel safe to learn. Try not to stop people as soon as they start messing up with TDD or write a bad design. See if you can give them time to learn from the mistake, and if they don't seem to be, ask some questions. Even wait until the retrospective before you say anything.

You need to foster the attitude that you're in the group but yet detached, able to observe the discussion and the code, and at the same time think about how to steer it. It's easier to do if you're not actually writing code yourself, although that makes it less fun for you. Sometimes it's just *so tempting* to step in, take over, implement a method, do a refactoring... It doesn't always work out well though. Your primary job is to create a conducive environment for learning, and it's hard to do that while you're concentrating on your own coding.

Dojo Disaster: But *I* can do it better!

One time I was facilitating a dojo, doing a Randori in Python. We were supposed to be practicing driving development with tests, and experiencing the rhythm of red-green-refactor. After a little while of coding, I could see we were getting somewhere with that, but the code wasn't as good as it could be. Python is my favourite programming language, and I could see that an ugly Java-like idiom was emerging. When the keyboard came round to me I just couldn't resist. I wanted to refactor that code and show off a cool dynamic programming technique (and my superior skills). I had 5 minutes to do it, and started hammering at the keyboard. The discussion turned towards python language features. People argued about the pros and cons of metaprogramming. Someone asked for an explanation of how my code actually worked, but I was too busy to talk to them. I eventually got my change to work and as the buzzer rang for the end of my timebox, passed on the keyboard with a happy sigh.

The code did look better, but at a cost. The group had totally lost the focus on experiencing TDD. My change needed quite a bit of explanation, and made us focus on the implementation code rather than what we'd intended to talk about - TDD. If I hadn't been so busy coding, I might have noticed what was going on, and just backed out my change. It wasn't *that* important, and actually, my skills weren't as superior as I thought! Next time I hope I'll keep a better sense of perspective, and be willing pass the keyboard right along to the next person.

It *is* less fun if you don't get to code though. You could try pair-facilitating, and cover for each other. If your group knows each other well, and is used to the dojo format, there may be less facilitation needed, too. For example in the Paris dojo they stress the responsibility of all participants to direct the meeting, and de-emphasize the facilitator role.

Ask Questions & Make Observations

I think it creates a more helpful atmosphere if you can frame your comments as questions or neutral observations. (This applies to everyone, not just the facilitator!) Say: *"Do you think it would make these tests more readable if we used a setUp method?"*, instead of telling people to do things: *"You need to extract that code into a setUp method!"*. Say: *"That test has two assert statements"*, rather than telling people off: *"Tests should only have one assert statement!"*.

This is a real art, and I learnt it from my daughter's violin teacher. She never tells my 8 year old she's playing it wrong. It's always *"which part of this melody should be quietest?"* or *"which open string should that note be the same as? Does it sound the same?"*. She never says *"you're too loud"* or *"you're flat"*, which is often what I'm thinking when I listen to her play! The art is to think *"you're flat"*, then before you open your mouth, work out how to phrase that as a question or neutral comment. Tricky to remember, but gets much better results!

Give Praise

If things are going well in your dojo, you should see some code that you like, and ways of working that you'd like to see more of. I usually applaud when we get an all-green test run, especially the first one! It becomes a regular pat on the back, encouraging us we're on the right track. If it seems appropriate, (and not patronizing), also congratulate people when they do something well. Praise is more useful the more specific it is, so say something like "good refactoring - nice small steps" or "that test reads well to me, it clearly follows arrange-act-assert." A plain "well done, good work!" is not wrong though.

Make notes

If you can spare some brainpower at the same time as doing all that, make notes. Jot down things you want to bring up in the retrospective later. I always aim to do this, but often when

I get to the retrospective, my notes are totally blank! It's a lot to hold in your head at once.

If someone asks difficult question or raises an issue that you don't want to address straight away, it can be a good idea to write it up on a piece of flipchart paper or a whiteboard placed where everyone can see. Use the heading "Parking Lot" to show that the issue is parked and not for discussion right now. It helps the person asking to feel heard, even though you're not answering them straight away. It also helps you remember the hard question and take it up again later, either at the retrospective or at a later meeting.

Facilitating particular coding activities

Exactly what the facilitator does is affected by the activities the group has chosen. Review the section "Collaborative Games for Programmers" for more information.

For a "Randori", there is a lot of managing discussions and ensuring people feel safe. I find it fun but quite stressful to do! For a "Randori in Pairs", it is quite different, and in some ways easier. You spend your time going from pair to pair, reading their code, asking questions and making suggestions. You have to read, understand and comment on a lot of code in a short space of time. It helps if you're already familiar with the kata they're working on.

If you've introduced a constraint game like "no conditionals" or "mute pairing", you have to help people to comply, and give them hints when they're stuck. When they complain, "But I have to use an 'if' statement here, there's no other way!" Your job is to say something like, "Well yes, it's not straightforward with the design you've chosen. Can you refactor it to use polymorphism instead?"

With a "Prepared Kata" session, your job is somewhat easier, since the pair at the front should have done some preparation, and will be steering the discussion. The facilitator role is to help managing the discussions, keep time, and offer constructive feedback in the retrospective.

Dojo Disaster: Only Say Nice Things

Do you remember that old advice - "Praise in public, criticise in private"? It's a good one to remember in your dojo! I was facilitating a Randori-in-Pairs one time, and the group was quite large, maybe 30 people. We'd been coding for about 90 minutes, and I'd been going around each pair in turn, reviewing code and discussing design choices. I hadn't got to each pair many times, but generally I was pretty pleased with what people had been coming up with. I called a halt for the retrospective, and asked if anyone wanted to share their code with the group. One pair volunteered, and brought their laptop to the front.

As their code went up on the big screen I quickly realized it must have been a while since I'd visited that pair! The code they showed had several obvious problems, some of which I'd already discussed with other pairs earlier in the session. My initial reaction was to point all those things out and start the discussion I'd normally have when coming up to a pair to review progress. Then thankfully some of my social skills kicked in! It rapidly dawned on me couldn't say all that stuff with everyone watching - no-one else would dare to show their code on the big screen afterwards!

So this is really a story about a dojo disaster averted. I made a rule for myself there and then - if you're showing some code to a group, only say nice things about it. It's the same in my daughter's violin class. For part of each lesson, two or three children in turn stand up infront of their peers and play a solo piece. After the mandatory applause, the teacher invites all the children in the group to make comments on the performance. The teacher is wise from many years of experience - she insists the children are only allowed to say **nice** things. Generally they come up with lots of good points - they get plenty of practice at giving positive feedback! Occasionally though, it's a struggle. Sometimes they're reduced to saying things like "she stood with her feet in the right places", or "he remembered to stop playing for the pause in the middle". So even when the music that came out was less than virtuoso standard, the performer will sit down feeling it's all ok, and they'll be willing to do it again the next time it's their turn.

Of course, in my dojo on this occasion, some of the other people sitting in the group could see the problems with the code up on the projector, since I'd observed them in their code earlier in the same session. So when I asked for another pair of volunteers to share, there were several respondents. As each one stepped up with their laptop, I was able to point out more and more good things about their code! I think the first pair quickly understood how they could make improvements. Thankfully I wasn't reduced to repeatedly putting a good face on it and pointing out how well everyone had done indenting their code, and remembering the language syntax.

The Retrospective

Your job in this part is firstly to make sure the retrospective happens. Coding is so much fun, the retrospective often gets squeezed out! More often than not someone is still trying to type even while the discussion is going on. It's so hard to leave code in an unfinished state, even when you know you're about to throw it away.

The facilitator has two main purposes in the retrospective. Firstly to get people to realize what they've learnt. You're more likely to remember the lessons of the dojo, and more likely to apply them in your daily coding, if you've actually articulated what they were. Your second purpose is to discuss what went less well so your next dojo will be even better!

Keep it friendly and safe for everyone to participate.

Prompting Discussions

There are some standard questions you can always ask to get the discussion moving:

- What are the best aspects of the design of the code we've ended up with?
- In what ways did we do Test Driven Development particularly well?
- Did we learn anything new?
- Did anything unexpected happen?
- What do we still need to practice more?
- What should we do differently in the next dojo?
- What will you do differently tomorrow in your production code?

Each kata in the catalogue in this book also has additional questions. When my notes are blank, (as they often are!) I find it really useful to have additional prompts.

It's about giving everyone a chance to say what they think is important, and to stop dominant individuals from hijacking the discussion.

You might find an open discussion difficult to manage, particularly with a larger group. You might want to do something more decentralized, as in this idea:

 Johannes Brodwall's tip

I end the dojo by asking everyone to write on stickies:

- one thing that surprised you
- one thing you learned
- one thing you plan to take with you

I collect the stickies and read out a few.

I end by telling everyone to take with them the "one thing you plan to take with you" sticky and put it in their pocket to remind themselves later.

At the original Paris dojo, they usually hold the retrospective at the start of the following meeting. The idea is partly that it gives you a week to calm down from all your passionate discussions about code. (!) It also lets you try out your improvement suggestions straight away, at that meeting. It does rely on it not being too long between meetings, and largely the same people coming every time though.

There are plenty more books out there about how to run a good retrospective, and being able to facilitate one is a useful skill to have. The dojo isn't the only place where a reflective discussion can lead to positive change.

At the end of your meeting, don't forget to thank everyone for coming into the dojo, and teaching and learning with you.

Planning for the next meeting

Hopefully the retrospective will have given you some ideas about what the group would like to work on next. It can be a good idea to repeat the same kata again the next time, you'll almost certainly gain new insights. Don't let it get stale or boring though. If someone has been inspired to do some more work on a kata after the dojo, perhaps ask them to prepare a kata performance for the next meeting. If you've done a refactoring kata, maybe try coding the same exercise again from scratch. Think about what skills people are still struggling with, and pick a different kata that will help you practice it. Also have a look at the section in this book Teaching & Learning In the Dojo.

Dojo Disaster: Innuendo

In which my fellow dojo participants took advantage of the fact that British humour is often based on embarrassment.

I was facilitating a dojo at an international conference, and I had asked four pairs of experienced programmers to each prepare a Kata to show to the group. The meeting

was going very well, we had seen some excellent coding
and pairing, and the group, (about 20 people), had been
asking lots of questions and giving useful feedback to the
presenters. The last pair stepped up to the keyboard, and
it soon became clear that they had planned to make their
coding episode a little more amusing, at my expense.
They began by explaining the "guiding test" for their
coding session, in the classic BDD format:

As an Emily,

I would like my transactions to be long enough

So that I am fully satisfied

It kind of went downhill from there, really!

To be fair, the pair did present some good code and tests,
including an explanation of the "Virtual Clock Pattern"[a],
and they were very charming about it. Everyone laughed
a lot, and I managed to laugh with them, despite feeling
acutely embarrassed. I think dojo facilitation is hard
enough as it is without other participants picking on you
for a joke!

---

[a]http://c2.com/cgi/wiki?VirtualClock

Handling Critical Voices

Sometimes in the Dojo, you'll find people start to question what's going on. They start to be critical, even hostile to the idea of practicing with Katas, ridicule the idea of Test Driven Development, and dismiss what you're doing as "messing about with toy code". People can get angry and make personal attacks. This can destroy the feeling of safety necessary for learning, at the same time as some criticisms are valid and need to be addressed.

The most important thing is to stay calm yourself, and keep treating everyone with respect, even if others are being rude. Try to be lighthearted, perhaps make a joke to try to defuse the tension. You could even try apologising. No really, even if you personally haven't done anything wrong, it can change the dynamic. (We British are very good at apologising, if you step on a British person's foot I can almost guarantee *they'll* say "sorry!").

You could remind people about the Dojo Principles. You could ask them to save their comments until the Retrospective, (by which time they'll have calmed down). You could write it up on the whiteboard as a "Parked topic" that you don't want to address right now. In the worst case, you could ask someone to leave the room, or break off the meeting altogether. Thankfully I've never yet found I needed to go that far.

Dojo Disaster: Herding cats

It was 2006, not long after Laurent Bossavit had visited my (then) workplace to teach us about the dojo, and I was really keen to try facilitating one. I discovered there was a newly-formed Gothenburg Ruby User Group, (a language I didn't actually know), and enthusiastically suggested to their leader (who I had never actually met) that we could do a dojo at the next meeting. Surprisingly, he agreed, and one rainy Wednesday evening after work, I met him at a small office above a shop somewhere on a Gothenburg backstreet. I set about reorganizing the furniture, while he set up his mac at the front, (a platform I'd never coded on). Shortly afterwards, roughly 20 ruby coders, (all of whom were men, few of whom I'd met before), turned up and started tucking into the free pizza on offer.

I talked a bit about the dojo idea, introduced the Kata, and then we started coding. I very rapidly learnt that the mac has a useful little key that looks rather like a swedish cinnamon bun. All sorts of exciting things happen if you instead try to copy and paste text using the "Ctrl" key! Thankfully in the end someone was also kind enough to tell me when the Python syntax I wrote didn't actually work in Ruby. I heaved a sigh of relief when the timer pinged for the end of my timebox driving, and I handed over the keyboard to the next person. For a while everything seemed to be going rather well, lots of people were talking, and tests and code were being written.

Then some people started asking challenging questions. Why are we writing tests? It would be much quicker/-better if we did it my way. This design sucks. 5 minutes is too short at the keyboard. I don't want to "fake it", why would I write something I'm just going to delete in a moment? I can write this code much better than (person who is currently driving), give me the keyboard! We should be using metaprogramming! (Instead of that boring code there that just made the tests pass). Have you seen my latest open source project? I've done this really cool thing...

I had never had to moderate this kind of discussion before, and I was lacking a lot of answers, shall we say. I was very glad when various of the more experienced Rubyists joined in, defending TDD and Refactoring and helping me keep the meeting on course. Thinking back, it was a kind of jostling for position and geek status, amongst a group of young programmers who didn't know each other very well. I didn't have the Randori Rules in place (I don't think they were invented then!) and I'd stepped well outside my comfort zone in a few too many places. At the time it felt very much like I'd spent the evening herding cats.

I survived, and lived to lead another dojo, but I wouldn't recommend it!

Common Objections

Here are some of the most common objections that come up, and some thoughts about how to handle them.

Code Katas are just toy code, they don't teach you anything useful.

Katas absolutely **are** toy code. It's not going into production, it's probably implemented better somewhere on the internet, and you'll likely throw your code away straight after the Dojo. That's why it's fun to work on!

Doing a Code Kata can absolutely teach you something. Learning new skills like TDD is hard. It's even harder if you're working on a real world coding problem you haven't faced before. Code Katas let you focus on everything *other* than delivering working code to customers. You can relax, try stuff out, make mistakes, throw it out and start over. If you experience the rhythm and flow of TDD in the ideal circumstances of a Code Kata, you might recognize that feeling when you get it in production code. You might even seek it out.

Why would I want to "Fake it" as a step in TDD? It doesn't make sense to write code I know I'm going to delete straight away.

If you can see what to write for the real solution, just write it! "Fake it" is a strategy in TDD to help you when you can't see the full, general thing to write straight away. It helps you via "Triangulation" to reach that general solution. In a code Kata it's often really easy to jump straight to the general solution, but the idea is, that we're practicing on easy code so we'll know what to do when things get tricky. Perhaps we could try that today?

Also re-read what Kent Beck writes about "Fake it 'til you make it" in his book "Test Driven Development by Example". (It's a Green Bar Pattern)

I can do TDD in Code Katas but it doesn't help me do it in my production code.

If you can do TDD in a Code Kata you're doing better than 99% of the programmers out there! Seriously! The step to doing it in your production code is probably about learning better design techniques. Some designs are inherently harder to test, and unfortunately there's a lot of that about. It could be that you've been practicing TDD on Katas where it's quite easy to find the tests to write and build up the design gradually, and your production code isn't like that. Have a look around the chapter in this book about Using Code Katas To Learn TDD. Try to find some Katas that help you practice around the problems you're seeing when trying to test drive your production code.

If you like, you could try bringing your production code into the dojo. Maybe someone there can help you see what to do differently. See the chapter on Using Production Code in the Dojo

Having said that, there are some situations when TDD is more difficult to do, or might not be the best choice. For example when designing multithreaded code. If you think you're in that kind of a situation, relax. Choose another testing approach, then try TDD again when the situation seems more appropriate.

You're taking such small steps! No-one codes like that in the real world, it would be too slow.

Yeah, I guess it might be a bit boring to watch someone coding so slowly. I think that's a big problem with good code, actually. It looks boring! The point is that sometimes you're working on really tricky code and you **do** need to take small steps. If you practice taking small steps on easy code, then you'll have a better chance of being able to do it when things get difficult. Actually, you can make very good progress even with small steps, and it's usually a less stressful way to work. Remember the fable of the tortoise and hare?

I don't believe TDD is a useful technique. I use better ways to produce good code.

If you have better ways to produce good code then I expect we'd all like to learn about them! Perhaps you could give us a prepared Kata demonstration sometime?

Actually, I'm a little bit skeptical when you say that you don't think TDD is a useful technique. I've heard some very good programmers use it, quite a lot of the time. Perhaps we should learn more about it before we decide. Can we spend the next few dojo meetings learning about TDD then reassess if we'd be better off moving on to other techniques?

Remember the Dojo Principle about mastery? If you're a master of some other technique, you may still find new knowledge and mastery together with others in the dojo. Please stay and we'll all learn something!

Section 3: Teaching & Learning In the Dojo

What could you learn in your dojo? That's one way of looking at it, but equally importantly - what could you teach? Everyone has different strengths, knowledge, and experience with various languages and tools. In the dojo you ought to meet people you can learn from in some areas, and teach in others. If you know something, being forced to explain it to a beginner can help you understand it even better, so you both teach and learn at the same time!

Skills like pair programming, reading other people's code, writing clean code, automated testing and articulating your ideas are the basis of everything that goes on in the dojo. At some meetings you might want to home in on particular skills or techniques. You might decide to do a kata you know well and have solved lots of times, in order to practice something else. For example, an unfamiliar programming language, editor, IDE, testing framework, or library.

Before I explain about these skills we want to learn in more detail, I'd like to go through the Dojo Principles. I love the way they are so succinct and Zen-like, and remind you that you come to the dojo in order to both teach and learn.

Later in this section I'll be talking a lot about which Code Katas to use while you're learning Test Driven Development, (TDD). This is one of the key skills you're trying to improve at in the dojo. In fact, one of the Dojo Principles says *"code without tests simply doesn't exist."*! I'll also talk about Katas that help you to learn about other styles of TDD, and Functional Programming. The remaining part of the section is a couple of essays I've written about what TDD actually is, and how to write good tests.

Dojo Principles

These principles were written by Christophe Thibaut, and first published in Laurent Bossavit's blog[20] in 2005, as a guide for new members of the first dojo, in Paris, France. (I have edited them in minor ways to improve readability.)

The First Rule

One important rule about the Dojo is : At the Dojo one can't discuss a form without code, and one can't show code without tests. It is a design training place, where it is acknowledged that "the code is the design" and that code without tests simply doesn't exist.

Finding a Master

The master can't be a master of every form. I feel quite at ease with recursive functions and list processing e.g. but I think I don't know how to create even a simple web app. Fortunately, while it's the first time they really deal with "tail-recursion" some practitioners here have done professional web apps for years!

Come Without Your Relics

Of course, you know how to do it. You know how and why this code is better than that one. You've done it already. The

---

[20]http://bossavit.com/dojo/archives/2005_02.html

point is to do it right now, explain it to us, and share what you learned.

Learning Again

In order to learn again something, we just have to forget it. But it's not easy to forget something when you're alone. It's easier when we give our full attention to someone who is trying to learn it for the first time. We can learn from other people's mistakes as well as from our own if we listen carefully.

Slow Down

Learning something should force you to slow down. You can go faster because you learned some tricks, but you cannot go faster and learn at the same time. It's OK, we're not in a hurry. We could do that for years. Some of us certainly will. What kind of deadline will we miss if we spend four more weeks on this code kata rather than on four different katas? More precisely, when we reach the next plateau, is it because we went through the previous one, or is it just because we were flying over it?

Throwing Yourself In

At some point someone will begin to master a particular Code Kata, and want to approach another one. Those threatened by boredom should throw themselves first into a Prepared Kata presentation.

Subjecting To A Master

If it seems difficult to you, look for other practitioners who can judge your code and could easily show something new about it to you. Ask again until the matter contains absolutely no more difficulty to you.

Mastering A Subject

If it seems easy to you, explain it to others who find it difficult. Explain it again as long as they find it difficult.

Using Code Katas to learn TDD

Test Driven Development is a multifaceted skill, that it takes study and practice to master. I think you can break it down into four closely related, and mutually supportive sub-skills:

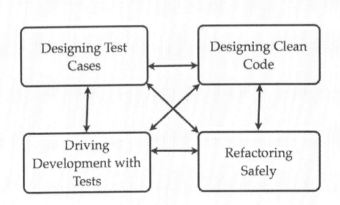

TDD sub-skills

When you're learning TDD it can help to "home in" on one or two of these sub-skills, and choose a Kata that challenges you more in that area. Here I've listed Katas that are good for each sub-skill, roughly in order of difficulty. Over a series of dojos, you could aim to do Katas which stretch you in each area in turn.

In addition, there are other styles of TDD that you can learn once you feel you're on top of the classic TDD skills. Perhaps the most well known is the London School of TDD. You could also look at Approval Testing, which can be particularly useful in the context of legacy code. If you're using a Functional programming style, you'll also find TDD working a little differently. In all these cases, I'd like to suggest some good Code Katas to work on.

Driving Development with Tests

This skill is about gradually building up a piece of code to solve a problem that's too big to solve in one go. You start with a Guiding Test as a goal, but that test should be too difficult to make pass in one step. You need to break down the problem into small pieces, identify test cases, and choose what order to implement them in. I think Kent Beck explains this process well in his book "Test Driven Development by Example". The process of working with a Guiding test in double-loop TDD is probably explained better in other texts, like "Growing Object Oriented Software, Guided by Tests", or "The RSpec book" by Chelimski et al.

When you're practicing these katas, see if you can begin with tests that only require a very simple implementation, but that should continue to pass even as you write more tests and build up an implementation for the whole problem.

All these katas are basically about building up an implementation of an algorithm gradually.

Easy:

- StringCalculator
- FizzBuzz
- Tennis

Medium to Hard:

- Prime Factors
- Yatzy
- Bowling Game
- Roman Numerals
- Potter

Katas that (probably) need more than one class to implement

If you want to practice building up an object graph, and incrementally designing the way responsibilities are divided between them, you might like to look at these katas.

- Medicine Clash
- Monty Hall
- Poker Hands
- Train Reservation

Refactoring Safely

This skill is about making a sequence of tiny, safe changes, that add up to a larger design improvement. The classic text on this is by Martin Fowler, "Refactoring: Improving the design of existing code".

All these katas have starting code that is less than clean, and your task is to improve the design without breaking the functionality. Some of these katas provide test cases, for others you also have to design the test cases you'll need to lean on while refactoring.

- Tennis
- Yatzy
- Gilded Rose
- Racing-Car Katas
- Trivia

Designing Test Cases

This skill is about designing test cases that cover the functionality, while at the same time being readable, robust and fast to execute. Beginners often enthusiastically write lots of tests, and later discover they are expensive to maintain, and rarely catch real problems. I've written about four Principles for Agile Automated Test Design elsewhere in this section. Alternatively, look at the "Three Pillars of Good Tests" from "The Art of Unit Testing" by Roy Osherove.

When you practice these katas, review your test cases carefully and discuss how well they follow the principles and/or pillars.

- Gilded Rose
- Minesweeper

- Game Of Life

Some code has challenges with external dependencies, and you need to isolate a small part in order to test it properly. Your test code might need to use a Test Double - a Mock, Stub or Fake. You can read more about Test Doubles in Gerard Meszaro's book "XUnit Patterns", and in my upcoming book "Mocks, Fakes and Stubs"[21].

You can use these katas to practice designing test cases that use a test double:

- Racing-Car Katas
- Monty Hall
- Medicine Clash
- Trivia
- Train Reservation

Designing Clean Code

This skill is about code that is readable, and makes good use of language idiom and style. For Java in particular, Robert Martin's book "Clean Code" is a pretty good guide. His book "Agile Software Development: Principles, Patterns and Practices" explains the SOLID design principles. Otherwise, a text like "Working Effectively with Legacy Code" by Michael Feathers talks a lot about good design, in the context of how to get to it from a poor one.

All Katas are suitable for practicing writing clean, readable code. These ones are particularly good:

---

[21]https://leanpub.com/mocks-fakes-stubs

- Args
- Racing-Car Katas
- Game of Life

London School TDD

London School TDD is as much an Object Oriented Programming design style as a testing approach. It was developed in London (!) by some early adopters of eXtreme Programming. Currently the best explanation of the technique is to be found in Steve Freeman and Nat Pryce's book *Growing Object Oriented Software, Guided by Tests.*

There is some discussion in the community about whether it is useful to learn London School TDD, or whether to just stick to Classic TDD. For a skilled developer, the code you come up with will be well designed and maintainable in either case. London School detractors also claim that there is no need to use mock objects, they are just a crutch for bad design, leading to complicated, brittle tests that don't prove anything useful.

Well, it seems to me that such an attitude is no fun at all! I find it rather interesting to study how different skilled TDD practitioners work. I want to know when they disagree with each other and why. I'm not content to have someone else tell me which style of TDD is best, I want to try them out for myself!

In order to practice London School TDD you need at least two classes. It's not so easy to use mocks to design an interface between a class and its collaborators, if that class has no collaborators! Many Code Katas only need you to write one class or one public method, and are not really suited to a London School approach.

I'd suggest these Katas are good for practicing London School TDD:

- Racing-Car Katas
- Medicine Clash
- Monty Hall
- Greenfield Gilded Rose
- Train Reservation

Approval Testing

Normally when you're doing TDD, you completely define the test up front, before you work on the implementation to make that test pass. Approval Testing changes the rules a little. You still fully define the "Arrange" and "Act" parts of the test up front, but only partially define the "Assert" part. You decide what behaviour you're going to assert on, but not exactly what that behaviour should be. You then go through an iterative process of developing the functionality and checking the actual output by hand, until you decide it's correct. Then you "Approve" the result and save it in the test. So the test is only fully defined once the implementation is finished.

Approval testing is an approach that needs good tools and good test design skills. There are lots of articles and videos available online, mostly around the tools "Approval Tests"[22] and "TextTest"[23]. There is also more information and a code kata example in my upcoming book "Mocks, Fakes and Stubs"[24].

---

[22]http://approvaltests.com

[23]http://texttest.org

[24]https://leanpub.com/mocks-fakes-stubs

In the Dojo you can try out Approval Testing for yourself, and find out more. I'd recommend these code katas:

- Minesweeper
- GildedRose
- Trivia

Functional Programming

Code Katas can be solved in many ways, and some lend themselves to a functional paradigm. If you'd like to learn a functional programming language, or just learn to use a more functional style in a multi-paradigm language like Python, there are some Katas that are better suited. Look for opportunities for recursion, and operations like map, filter, sum. Also think carefully about datastructures and how to handle state.

If you're coming from an Object-Oriented background, and diving into learning a totally new language like Clojure or Haskell, you might like to start with a very simple kata that you already know well. I'd suggest something like String Calculator, before moving on to some of these other katas.

If you'd like to learn more about Functional programming, you might like the book "Functional Programming for the Object-Oriented Programmer" by Brian Marick.

I'd recommend practicing these katas in a functional style:

- Bank OCR
- Game of Life
- Reversi

TDD in terms of States and Moves

People often use Robert Martin's "3 rules"[25] to explain TDD:

1. You are not allowed to write any production code unless it is to make a failing unit test pass.
2. You are not allowed to write any more of a unit test than is sufficient to fail; and compilation failures are failures.
3. You are not allowed to write any more production code than is sufficient to pass the one failing unit test.

Although this is undoubtedly a correct description, I find it a little terse and fierce to use with complete beginners. I want people to feel safe in the dojo, and have instructions that help tell them positively what they should be doing.

Dojo Disaster: Facepalm

I was facilitating a dojo for a small group, where a couple of the people hadn't even heard of TDD before. We were doing a Randori, with Ping-Pong switching. After we'd been coding only a little while, someone slightly more experienced wrote a failing test, then handed the keyboard to one of these beginners. The beginner looks puzzled and starts reading the code. "What should I do?"

[25]http://butunclebob.com/ArticleS.UncleBob.TheThreeRulesOfTdd

he asks. "Do the simplest thing possible to make the test pass!" comes the suggestion. So he goes to the test code, finds the failing test, and changes the "expected" value in the assertEquals to match the "actual" value. "Look! it passes!". (Collective facepalm).

So that's what gave me the idea for TDD in terms of states and moves. When you're in the Red state, generally the only valid moves involve changing the *production* code. I've found explaining this beforehand reduces embarrassment at the keyboard.

My preferred way to explain TDD to beginners uses the picture below. Most people will be familiar with the Red-Green-Refactor cycle, but I've also added an "Overview" state.

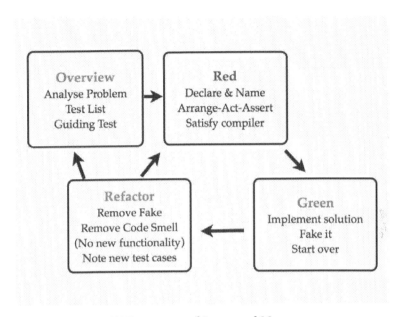

TDD in terms of States and Moves

In the Dojo, if there are TDD beginners present, I'll normally sketch this picture up on a whiteboard before we start coding. As I write each state, I'll explain a bit about what I mean. Let me take you through my TDD explanation.

Overview State

Before you start coding, I think it pays to step back a little and try to analyse the problem we're trying to solve. Not long - we don't want analysis paralysis or Big Design Up Front. In the Dojo, when you get to the coding part, I'd suggest actually spending up to 15 minutes talking about the chosen Kata before writing much (any!) code. You need to help everyone understand the problem you're planning to solve together. Start by sketching and noting test cases on the whiteboard.

In the **Overview** state you:

- Make a basic analysis of the problem.
- Review any existing code in the area and identify where the new functionality will be called from.
- Go back to the Customer/Product Owner and ask questions.
- Write a Guiding Test.
- Make a list of other (smaller) test cases, and think about what order to implement them in.

Move on to the next state - **Red** - when:

- You understand your goal for the coding session & have chosen your next test

Clarifications

The Customer or Product Owner is the person you as a developer talk to in order to clarify requirements. In the Dojo, usually the facilitator takes this role.

A "Guiding Test" is a test that will pass when you're done with your coding session, but is too big to make pass straight away. It gives you a goal for your session, and is usually a non-trivial example use for your User Story or Kata. Sometimes people call it a "Coaching Test" since it should coach you into the right frame of mind to tackle the problem. Others call it an "Acceptance Test" since it can reflect acceptance criteria for a User Story. Still others prefer to call it a "Story Test" since it is a test for a whole User Story. In Behaviour Driven Development it could be a Scenario expressed as a unit test.

Red state

You're trying to set up a small, achievable goal. Choose a test from your list, that will help you towards your session goal (Guiding Test), or will force you to address a weakness in your current production code. If you've just made a fake to get the last test to pass, this next test should force you to remove it (via what Kent Beck calls "triangulation"[26]).

In the **Red** state you:

- Declare and name a test
- Arrange - Act - Assert (start by writing the Assert)
- Add just enough production code to satisfy the compiler (if you have one)

Move on to the next state - **Green** - when:

- Your test describes the missing functionality, executes, and fails.

Clarifications

When writing the test name, you might find it helpful to use this template:

- method_name_With_arguments_Returns_return_value()

for example:

---
[26]in his book "Test-Driven Development by Example"

- add_With_Empty_String_Returns_Zero()

(Which could be the first test in the StringCalculator Kata)

Remembering the 3 'A's "Arrange - Act - Assert" helps you to structure your actual test code. Bill Wake invented the idea, and wrote an article that I think explains it well: "3A - Arrange, Act, Assert"[27]

Green state

You're trying to get the new test to pass as soon as possible, even if that means taking shortcuts with the design. Copy and paste code if you must. Make a long method even longer. Fake it. On the other hand, if you can see how to do it right, just do it. Just don't take too long over it. You should try to never be more than a few minutes away from having all the tests passing. Even if that means deleting all the code and the test you just wrote.

- Change the production code - implement just enough to make the test pass
- Fake it (if you're unsure)
- When all else fails, remove the failing test, get back to green, and write an easier test.

Move on to the next state - **Refactor** - when:

- Your tests all execute and **pass**

---

[27]http://xp123.com/articles/3a-arrange-act-assert/

Refactor state

Now you have the system working, make it right. Remove duplication and other code smells. Take small steps so you are never more than a few keystrokes from having all the tests passing. Don't forget to also refactor the test code to the same standard as the production code.

- Change production code: remove fakes, code smells
- Change test code: improve readability
- Don't add functionality not required by tests.
- You might think of new test cases while you're refactoring - note them on your list.
- Run the tests after each refactoring. They should continue to pass.

Move on to the next state - **Red** or **Overview** - when:

- The code is clean and your tests all execute and pass.
- Move to the "Red" state if you already know the next test to write. Otherwise move to the "Overview" state.

Clarifications

While you're refactoring, you might make a mistake. In this case hopefully the tests will alert you by failing. In this case the safest thing to do is just to undo all your recent changes until you get back to passing tests. If you can easily see the mistake you've made though, do go ahead and just fix the problem. If you can't quickly see the problem, and start hacking about, you're on a slippery slope. Hopefully your pairing partner won't let you continue sliding down it, but will force you to back out your failed refactoring to get quickly back to the solid ground of passing tests.

While you're refactoring, you will probably spot weaknesses in the code - functionality that is still missing, or maybe hard coded fakes we forgot about. Note these things down as tests on the list. If you fix them straight off the danger is you won't have test coverage for the increased functionality.

When to stop

At some point hopefully you'll get your guiding test to pass, and you'll be happy with the design of your code. Often in the dojo, the time runs out for coding before this happens. Try to resist the temptation to skip the retrospective and just keep coding. It's important to reflect on what's happened and discuss what you'd do differently if you did this exercise again. At your next dojo, you can always do the same Kata again. You'll start from scratch of course, but you should get further since you've learnt more about the exercise.

Principles for Agile Automated Test Design

Once you've worked on a system with extensive automated tests, I don't think you'll want to go back to working without them. You get this incredible sense of freedom to change the code, refactor, and keep making frequent releases to end users.

Actually, you design automated functional tests for two main purposes. Initially you want to clarify your understanding of what to build. In fact, at that point they're not really tests, you usually call them scenarios, or examples. Later, the main purpose of the tests becomes to detect regression errors, although you continue use them to document what the system does.

When I'm designing a test case for a particular piece of functionality, I want to assess whether it will document that functionality and provide regression protection, whilst being cost effective to write and maintain. As with most software, it's the maintenance cost that will dominate. The four principles outlined below help me to design better, more maintainable tests.

Readability

When you look at the test case, you can read it through and understand what the test is for. You can see what the expected behaviour is, and what aspects of it are covered by the test. When the test fails, you can quickly see what is broken.

If your test case is not readable, it will not be useful, neither for understanding what the system does, or identifying regression errors. When it fails you will have to dig though other sources outside of the test case to find out what is wrong. Quite likely you will not understand what is wrong and you will rewrite the test to check for something else, or simply delete it.

Robustness

When a test fails, it means there is a regression error, (functionality is broken), or the system has changed and the tests no longer document the correct behaviour. You need to take action to correct the system or update the test, and this is as it should be. If however, the test has failed for no good reason, you have a problem: a fragile test.

There are many causes of fragile tests. For example tests that are not isolated from one another, duplication between test cases, and dependencies on random or threaded code. If you run a test by itself and it passes, but fails in a suite together with other tests, then you have an isolation problem. If you have one broken feature and it causes a large number of test failures, you have duplication between test cases. If you have a test that fails in one test run, then passes in the next when nothing changed, you have a flickering test.

If your tests often fail for no good reason, you will start to ignore them. Quite likely there will be real failures hiding amongst all the false ones, and the danger is you will not see them.

Speed

As an agile developer you run your test suite frequently. Both (a) every time you build the system, (b) before you check in changes, and (c) after check-in in an automated Continuous Integration environment. I recommend time limits of 2 minutes for (a), 10 minutes for (b), and 60 minutes for (c). This fast feedback gives you the best chance of actually being willing to run the tests, and to find defects when they're cheapest to fix, soon after insertion.

If your test suite is slow, it will not be used. When you're feeling stressed, you'll skip running them, and problem code will enter the system. In the worst case the test suite will never become green. You'll fix the one or two problems in a given run and kick off a new test run, but in the meantime you'll continue developing and making other changes. The diagnose-and-fix loop gets longer and the tests become less likely to ever all pass at the same time. This can become pretty demoralizing.

Updatability

When the needs of the users change, and the system is updated, your tests also need to be updated in tandem. It should be straightforward to identify which tests are affected by a given change, and quick to update them all.

If your tests are not easy to update, they will likely get left behind as the system moves on. Faced with a small change that causes thousands of failures and hours of work to update them all, you'll likely delete most of the tests.

Following these four principles implies Maintainability

Taken all together, I think how well your tests adhere to these principles will determine how maintainable they are, or in other words, how much they will cost. That cost needs to be in proportion to the benefits you get: helping you understand what the system does, and regression protection.

As your test suite grows, it becomes more challenging to adhere to all the principles. Readability suffers when there are so many test cases you can't see the forest for the trees. The more details of your system that you cover with tests, the more likely you are to have Robustness problems - tests that fail when these details change. Speed obviously also suffers - the time to run the test suite usually scales linearly with the number of test cases. Updatability doesn't necessarily get worse as the number of test cases increases, but it will if you don't adhere to good design principles in your test code, or lack tools for bulk update of test data for example.

How can you use these principles in the dojo?

I find it useful to remember these principles when designing test cases. I may need to make tradeoffs between them, and it helps just to step back and assess how I'm doing on each principle from time to time as I develop. If I'm reviewing someone's test cases in the dojo, I can point to code and say which principles it's not following, and give them concrete advice about how to make improvements. We can have a discussion for example about whether to add more test cases in order to improve regression protection, and how to do that without reducing overall readability.

I think the principles are largely the same whether you're writing skinny little unit tests or fatter functional tests that touch more of the codebase. My experience tells me that it's a lot easier to be successful with unit tests. As the testing thickness increases, the feedback cycle gets slower, and your mistakes are amplified. That's why I concentrate on teaching these principles through unit testing exercises in the dojo. Once you understand what you're aiming for, you can transfer your skills to functional tests.

Other Principles

In his book "The Art of Unit Testing", Roy Osherove talks about "Three Pillars of Good Tests", which I'd summarize like this:

- **Trustworthiness**: test results are accurate, developers will accept them with confidence.
- **Maintainability**: tests are easy and quick to update when code changes.
- **Readability**: you can easily and correctly interpret test failures.

Obviously we agree on the importance of Readability, and his description of Maintainability largely matches mine for Updatability. I think his Trustworthiness pillar is similar to Robustness. If you prefer to think about the three pillars instead of four principles, then don't let me stop you! I think our goal is the same.

Section 4: Kata Catalogue

There are many, many code katas, and this catalogue is in no way exhaustive. These are some of my favourites, and ones which I've found to work well in the context of a coding dojo.

What is a Code Kata?

A Code Kata is a small, fun problem that shouldn't take you more than an hour or two to solve in your favourite programming language. The rule is that you must repeat the exercise, and every time try to improve the way you solve the problem. Not just the code you end up with, but the process by which you get to it.

I don't think learning a code kata has anything to do with learning a sequence of keystrokes or perfectly imitating some kind of "master" programmer. That's where the analogy with Karate breaks down! When you "know" a kata, that means that solving the actual problem no longer presents any difficulty to you, and you can concentrate on improving all the other aspects of *how* you solve it. You'll be able to try out a variety of approaches: object oriented, functional languages, big tests, small tests, another order of tests, with and without faking it, refactoring at this point or that point, different datastructures, algorithms, names... Every time you do the kata, you can try out something new, or make a small improvement to an approach you've used before.

Dojo Disaster: The Architect's Kata

Emmanuel Gaillot recounted for me an incident when somebody new turned up to the Paris dojo. He described himself as a "software architect", and he suggested that not all katas need involve coding. He instead proposed a "design" kata. The group discussed the idea, and the fact that they'd set up the dojo as a place where you learn by **coding** infront of others. On the other hand, someone suggested that in order to really understand a rule, maybe you should break it and see what you can learn.

So they decided to take up the architect's suggestion, and spent an evening drawing boxes and arrows. It didn't turn out so well. As Emmanuel put it: "It was excruciating!". Everyone agreed it was not fun at all. So they kept the rule about coding - in fact, all the Katas in this catalogue involve writing code.

So I agree with Emmanuel, (see the Sidebar "The Architect's Kata"), a code kata must also involve writing actual code. And tests!

How to choose a good Kata for your dojo

The most important thing is to choose a Kata you will enjoy doing! Flip through the catalogue and pick out any topics that look interesting. Have a look at the section "Contexts to use this Kata" for an idea of what you might learn from it. If there is a skill you're working on, there is some advice in the previous section "Teaching & Learning In the Dojo", with suggestions of which Katas are particularly useful.

About this Catalogue

Each Kata has an explanation of the problem to be solved, and links to where you can download starting code (if applicable). In addition, I've added some suggestions to help you get the most out of the kata, and to choose one appropriate for your context.

Additional discussion points for the Retrospective

After you've done the kata, these questions might prompt interesting discussion. (You might be having a great discussion anyway, of course!) When I'm facilitating a dojo, I often find the retrospective is the hardest part. I can see that the group has learnt lots through doing the Kata, but I don't always know how to get people talking about it. That's why I've written these extra notes, to remind me of some questions that might spark good discussion.

Ideas for after the Dojo

If you've done this kata in a dojo, you might be inspired to try it again by yourself at home. Here are some ideas for how to extend the kata or vary it in some way, so you get the most out of it. If several dojo participants continue to work on a kata after the dojo, you can go online to share code snippets, ideas and links, and to continue to discuss what was said in the meeting. Alternatively you could share what you've learnt at the next dojo meeting.

Contexts to use this Kata

If you're in a particular situation, any individual kata might be more or less suitable. This section should help you to choose a good Kata, and help you prepare for your dojo meeting.

Kata: Args[28]

Most of us have had to parse command-line arguments from time to time. If we don't have a convenient utility, then we simply walk the array of strings that is passed into the main function. There are several good utilities available from various sources, but they probably don't do exactly what we want. So let's write another one!

The arguments passed to the program consist of flags and values. Flags should be one character, preceded by a minus sign. Each flag should have zero, or one value associated with it.

You should write a parser for this kind of arguments. This parser takes a **schema** detailing what arguments the program expects. The schema specifies the number and types of flags and values the program expects.

Once the schema has been specified, the program should pass the actual argument list to the args parser. It will verify that the arguments match the schema. The program can then ask the args parser for each of the values, using the names of the flags. The values are returned with the correct types, as specified in the schema.

For example if the program is to be called with these arguments:

---

[28]With thanks to Robert C. Martin, who designed this Kata, for permission to include it here.

```
-l -p 8080 -d /usr/logs
```

this indicates a schema with 3 flags: l, p, d. The "l" (logging) flag has no values associated with it, it is a boolean flag, True if present, False if not. the "p" (port) flag has an integer value, and the "d" (directory) flag has a string value.

If a flag mentioned in the schema is missing in the arguments, a suitable default value should be returned. For example "False" for a boolean, 0 for a number, and "" for a string.

If the arguments given do not match the schema, it is important that a good error message is given, explaining exactly what is wrong.

If you are feeling ambitious, extend your code to support lists eg

```
-g this,is,a,list -d 1,2,-3,5
```

So the "g" flag indicates a list of strings, ["this", "is", "a", "list"] and the "d" flag indicates a list of integers, [1, 2, -3, 5].

Make sure your code is extensible, in that it is straightforward and obvious how to add new types of values.

Notes:

- What the schema should look like and how to specify it is deliberately left vague in the Kata description. An important part of the Kata is to design a concise yet readable format for it.
- Make sure you have a test with a negative integer (confusing - sign)

- The order of the arguments need not match the order given in the schema.
- Don't forget to check suitable default values are correctly assigned if flags given in the schema are missing in the args given.

Additional discussion points for the Retrospective

- Compare your API with the API of the standard command line argument parsing package you'd normally use in your language.
- Is your error handling code hiding the logic of the main flow? (You do have error handling code, right?)

Ideas for after the Dojo

In Robert C. Martin's book "Clean Code" there is a full worked solution written in Java. He mentions in a footnote on page 200 that he has also solved it in Ruby. The code is available on his github page here for Java[29], and here for Ruby[30]. Review the code. How can the Ruby version be so much smaller?

Try the Kata again yourself in a different programming language. Did it turn out smaller than the first time? Cleaner?

Contexts to use this Kata

This Kata is about writing a simple parser, and designing a library API. Other Katas that involve parsing strings are for example StringCalculator and BankOCR.

[29]http://github.com/unclebob/javaargs
[30]http://github.com/unclebob/rubyargs

If you're reading the book "Clean Code" by Robert C. Martin, I recommend you do this kata for yourself before you read the chapter on it in the book. I think this Kata is interesting to do in different kinds of programming languages and compare your choices of api and schema definition. Also compare the readability/size of the code you end up with.

Kata: Bank OCR

User Story 1

You work for a bank, which has recently purchased a spiffy machine to assist in reading letters and faxes sent in by branch offices. The machine scans the paper documents, and produces a file with a number of entries which each look like this:

```
    _  _     _  _  _  _  _
  | _| _||_||_ |_   ||_||_|
  ||_  _|  | _||_|  ||_| _|
```

Each entry is 4 lines long, and each line has 27 characters. The first 3 lines of each entry contain an account number written using pipes and underscores, and the fourth line is blank. Each account number should have 9 digits, all of which should be in the range 0-9. A normal file contains around 500 entries.

Your first task is to write a program that can take this file and parse it into actual account numbers.

User Story 2

Having done that, you quickly realize that the spiffy machine is not in fact infallible. Sometimes it goes wrong in its scanning. The next step therefore is to validate that the numbers you read are in fact valid account numbers. A valid account number has a valid checksum. This can be calculated as follows:

```
account number:  3  4  5  8  8  2  8  6  5
position names:  d9 d8 d7 d6 d5 d4 d3 d2 d1
```

checksum calculation:

$$(d1+2*d2+3*d3 + .. +9*d9) \bmod 11 = 0$$

So now you should also write some code that calculates the checksum for a given number, and identifies if it is a valid account number.

User Story 3

Your boss is keen to see your results. He asks you to write out a file of your findings, one for each input file, in this format:

```
457508000
664371495 ERR
86110??36 ILL
```

ie the file has one account number per row. If some characters are illegible, they are replaced by a ?. In the case of a wrong checksum, or illegible number, this is noted in a second column indicating status.

User Story 4

It turns out that often when a number comes back as ERR or ILL it is because the scanner has failed to pick up on one pipe or underscore for one of the figures. For example

The 9 could be an 8 if the scanner had missed one |. Or the 0 could be an 8. Or the 1 could be a 7. The 5 could be a 9 or 6. So your next task is to look at numbers that have come back as ERR or ILL, and try to guess what they should be, by adding or removing just one pipe or underscore. If there is only one possible number with a valid checksum, then use that. If there are several options, the status should be AMB. If you still can't work out what it should be, the status should be reported ILL.

Additional discussion points for the Retrospective

- How readable are your test cases? Can you look at them and easily see which digits are being parsed?
- What would happen if the input changed format to 12 digits instead of 9? How well would your code cope?

Ideas for after the Dojo

This Kata is too big for just one meeting, you'll probably need several to get to all four parts. If you're interested in experimenting with a functional paradigm, try this Kata both with iteration and recursion.

Contexts to use this Kata

The first part of this Kata is about parsing, and there are other Katas that also do so, for example Minesweeper, Args.

The second and third parts are mostly about making your calculation code clear and concise, and reflect the domain language of the problem. The fourth part is a little more challenging, and you need to think clearly about the algorithm you want to use to search for alternative legal solutions.

Kata: Bowling Game[31]

Create a program, which, given a valid sequence of rolls for one line of American Ten-Pin Bowling, produces the total score for the game. This is a summary of the rules of the game:

- Each game, or "line" of bowling, includes ten turns, or "frames" for the bowler.
- In each frame, the bowler gets up to two tries to knock down all the pins.
- If in two tries, he fails to knock them all down, his score for that frame is the total number of pins knocked down in his two tries.
- If in two tries he knocks them all down, this is called a "spare" and his score for the frame is ten plus the number of pins knocked down on his next throw (in his next turn).
- If on his first try in the frame he knocks down all the pins, this is called a "strike". His turn is over, and his score for the frame is ten plus the simple total of the pins knocked down in his next two rolls.
- If he gets a spare or strike in the last (tenth) frame, the bowler gets to throw one or two more bonus balls, respectively. - These bonus throws are taken as part of the same turn. If the bonus throws knock down all the pins, the process does not repeat: the bonus throws are only used to calculate the score of the final frame.

---

[31]With thanks to Robert C. Martin, who designed this Kata, for permission to include it here.

- The game score is the total of all frame scores.

Here are some things that the program will not do:

- We will not check for valid rolls.
- We will not check for correct number of rolls and frames.
- We will not provide scores for intermediate frames.

The input is a scorecard from a finished bowling game, where "X" stands for a strike, "-" for no pins bowled, and "/" means a spare. Otherwise figures 1-9 indicate how many pins were knocked down in that throw.

Sample games:

123451234512345

always hitting pins without getting spares or strikes, a total score of 60

XXXXXXXXXXXX

a perfect game, 12 strikes, giving a score of 300

9-9-9-9-9-9-9-9-9-9-

heartbreak - 9 pins down each round, giving a score of 90

5/5/5/5/5/5/5/5/5/5/5

a spare every round, giving a score of 150

Additional discussion points for the Retrospective

- Did you do any design before you started coding? If so, does your code have this design now?
- At what point did you realize you can't simply loop over frames, that you in fact need to refer to the previous frame as well as the current one in order to calculate the score? In an ideal world, when should you have realized this?
- Look at the code you have ended up with, and compare it with the above description of the rules of bowling. Is there any similarity in the words used in each?
- Did you do enough refactoring? How would you know?
- How did you decide which tests to write, and in which order? Did it matter what order you implemented them in?

Ideas for after the Dojo

Read this article "Engineer Notebook: An Extreme Programming Episode"[32] by Robert C. Martin, where he describes solving this kata together with Robert S. Koss. Follow along in your editor. Does he do the kata the same way as you would?

---

[32]http://www.objectmentor.com/resources/articles/xpepisode.htm

Contexts to use this Kata

This kata is relatively easy for newcomers to TDD. It's a good one for creating a test list at the start, and choosing a suitable order to implement them in that allows the algorithm to develop organically.

As Robert Martin points out in his article, it is possible to analyse the requirements for this problem and come up with an over-designed solution. If you do this Kata with TDD newcomers it could show them how TDD can help you discover a good design for your software without too much up-front work.

Kata: FizzBuzz

Imagine the scene. You are eleven years old, and in the five minutes before the end of the lesson, your Maths teacher decides he should make his class more "fun" by introducing a "game". He explains that he is going to point at each pupil in turn and ask them to say the next number in sequence, starting from one. The "fun" part is that if the number is divisible by three, you instead say "Fizz" and if it is divisible by five you say "Buzz". So now your maths teacher is pointing at all of your classmates in turn, and they happily shout "one!", "two!", "Fizz!", "four!", "Buzz!"... until he very deliberately points at you, fixing you with a steely gaze... time stands still, your mouth dries up, your palms become sweatier and sweatier until you finally manage to croak "Fizz!". Doom is avoided, and the pointing finger moves on.

So of course in order to avoid embarrassment in front of your whole class, you have to get the full list printed out so you know what to say. Your class has about 33 pupils and he might go round three times before the bell rings for breaktime. Next maths lesson is on Thursday. Get coding!

Write a program that prints the numbers from 1 to 100. But for multiples of three print "Fizz" instead of the number and for the multiples of five print "Buzz". For numbers which are multiples of both three and five print "FizzBuzz".

Sample output:

```
1
2
Fizz
4
Buzz
Fizz
7
8
Fizz
Buzz
11
Fizz
13
14
FizzBuzz
16
17
Fizz
19
Buzz
```

... etc up to 100

Additional discussion points for the Retrospective

- Is the code you have written clean? Are there any smells?
- Did you refactor throughout or do it all at the end?
- What if a new requirement came along that multiples of seven were "Whizz"? Could you add that without editing the existing code? (Cue discussion of the Open-Closed Principle)

Ideas for after the Dojo

- When you've got it all working for "Fizz" and "Buzz", add "Whizz" for multiples of seven
- Then add "Fizz" also for all numbers containing a 3 (eg 23, 53)

Contexts to use this Kata

I find this an excellent kata for introducing beginners to TDD. It's pretty straightforward to choose the order of test cases, work in small steps, and complete the whole exercise still leaving time for a decent retrospective.

Kata: Game Of Life

The Game of Life is a cellular automaton devised by the British mathematician John Horton Conway in 1970. It's a zero-player game, meaning that its evolution is determined by its initial state, requiring no further input - you create an initial configuration and watch how it evolves. Some initial patterns give rise to complex and beautiful ever-changing scenarios, others eventually stabilize into a fixed configuration.

The universe of the Game of Life is an infinite two-dimensional orthogonal grid of square cells, each of which is in one of two possible states, alive or dead. Every cell interacts with its eight neighbours, which are the cells that are horizontally, vertically, or diagonally adjacent. At each step in time, the following transitions occur:

- Any live cell with fewer than two live neighbours dies, as if caused by under-population.
- Any live cell with two or three live neighbours lives on to the next generation.
- Any live cell with more than three live neighbours dies, as if by overcrowding.
- Any dead cell with exactly three live neighbours becomes a live cell, as if by reproduction.

The initial pattern constitutes the seed of the system. The first generation is created by applying the above rules simultaneously to every cell in the seed — births and deaths occur simultaneously, and the discrete moment at which this happens is sometimes called a tick (in other words, each generation is a pure function of the preceding one). The rules continue to be applied repeatedly to create further generations.

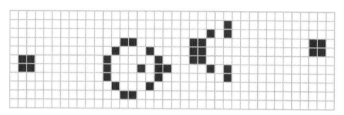

Gosper Glider Gun (image from wikipedia)

This aim of this Kata is to write some code that calculates the following generations, given a starting "seed" position. For example, you could start with the "glider gun", above, and see it generate a stream of gliders in subsequent turns. It's also pretty cool if you can manage to write code to visualize the cells as the position changes after each new generation.

Additional discussion points for the Retrospective

- Did you start with a "Cell" class or a "World" class? Or the "tick" function? How did that initial decision affect the code you ended up with?
- Did you find a good datastructure to represent an infinite two-dimensional orthogonal grid?
- What would happen if the requirements changed now and instead of two-dimensional, the grid became three-dimensional? Is the knowledge about x, y coordinates spread all over your code and in all the method signatures?

- How well does your code reflect the domain language of the problem? For example do you have the concept of a "tick" or a "seed" or a "generation" in your code?

Ideas for after the Dojo

This is the most popular kata done at Code Retreat events, and a lot of people have done it. There are lots of screencasts and blog posts about it that you could look at.

If you do the kata again, try starting from a different place. If you started with a "Cell" class, try starting with a "tick" function. Or try starting with the visualization of the next generations. Or with parsing an ASCII art representation of the seed. Or create a clickable grid for people to input their seed. There are lots of aspects to this Kata, and in one dojo you won't have explored all the possibilities.

Contexts to use this Kata

This is a good Kata for a functional programming style. It's also good for thinking about using domain language in code. There are other katas that use a two dimensional grid, you might find it interesting to compare this one with Minesweeper and Reversi.

Kata: Gilded Rose[33]

Hi and welcome to team Gilded Rose. As you know, we are a small inn with a prime location in a prominent city ran by a friendly innkeeper named Allison. We also buy and sell only the finest goods. Unfortunately, our goods are constantly degrading in quality as they approach their sell by date. We have a system in place that updates our inventory for us. It was developed by a no-nonsense type named Leeroy, who has moved on to new adventures. Your task is to add the new feature to our system so that we can begin selling a new category of items. First an introduction to our system:

- All items have a SellIn value which denotes the number of days we have to sell the item
- All items have a Quality value which denotes how valuable the item is
- At the end of each day our system lowers both values for every item

Pretty simple, right? Well this is where it gets interesting:

- Once the sell by date has passed, Quality degrades twice as fast
- The Quality of an item is never negative

---

[33]With thanks to Terry Hughes, who originally designed this Kata, for permission to include it here.

- "Aged Brie" actually increases in Quality the older it gets
- The Quality of an item is never more than 50
- "Sulfuras", being a legendary item, never has to be sold or decreases in Quality
- "Backstage passes", like aged brie, increases in Quality as it's SellIn value approaches; Quality increases by 2 when there are 10 days or less and by 3 when there are 5 days or less but Quality drops to 0 after the concert

We have recently signed a supplier of conjured items. This requires an update to our system:

- "Conjured" items degrade in Quality twice as fast as normal items

Feel free to make any changes to the UpdateQuality method and add any new code as long as everything still works correctly. However, do not alter the Item class or Items property as those belong to the goblin in the corner who will insta-rage and one-shot you as he doesn't believe in shared code ownership (you can make the UpdateQuality method and Items property static if you like, we'll cover for you).

Just for clarification, an item can never have its Quality increase above 50, however "Sulfuras" is a legendary item and as such its Quality is 80 and it never alters.

Original Kata: Legacy C Sharp

In the original version of this Kata, there were no tests provided, only a textual description of the requirements, (above), and some smelly looking C#, which you can download from Bobby Johnson's repo on GitHub[34]. The idea is to practice handling a legacy system, where you take this less than clean code, and transform it via small steps into something that can be maintained and extended. The proof that you have the code under control, is that you can easily add the new feature: "Conjured" items.

I've taken the original kata and extended it so you can practice more things with it. I will explain more about each of the variants in the following sections.

Kata variant #1: Design in different languages

I've translated the original code into a number of different programming languages, (with a little help from my friends!). You can find the code in my github repo[35]. The aim is to practice good design using a particular programming language and tools. First you need to design tests that you can lean on when you start refactoring. Then you can find out how good your tests are by using them when refactoring the code. Then you can find out how good your refactored design is by adding the new feature for Conjured items.

Note that my C# version of the code is slightly different from the original, since it is designed to present the same challenges as the other translations. Not all the original C# idioms translated well. Also, if you're doing this variant, you should ignore the text-based approval tests for the code which are also in the repo.

---

[34]https://github.com/NotMyself/GildedRose
[35]https://github.com/emilybache/GildedRose-Refactoring-Kata

Kata variant #2: Test Design and Tool Choice

How does it change things if you use a different kind of testing tool or approach? You could divide the dojo participants into pairs, and have each trying out a different tool.

Example tools:

- a unit testing framework like JUnit[36]
- a BDD framework like RSpec[37]
- a functional test framework like Cucumber[38] or Fitnesse[39].
- an approval testing framework like Approval Tests[40] or TextTest[41]

You can compare how well you can use the domain language of the problem to express the tests in each. Perhaps introduce an error in your code and look at the failure information you get. Would that help you find and correct the problem quickly and easily? See also the "Principles for Agile Automated Test Design").

---

[36]http://junit.org

[37]http://rspec.info/

[38]http://cukes.info/

[39]http://fitnesse.org/

[40]http://approvaltests.sourceforge.net/

[41]http://texttest.org

Kata variant #3: Refactor using Approval Tests

Instead of writing all the tests yourself, you could try using the approval tests I've provided, (found in the repo in the subfolder "texttests"). This lets you concentrate on the Refactoring part of the Kata. I've provided test fixtures that let you run the same tests against each language version of the kata. The text-based tests give you full branch and statement coverage of the code, and are designed to be used with the open source tool TextTest[42]. There is more information about how to do this in the README file in the "texttests" folder.

I wouldn't recommend using an approval testing approach without tool support. The command line version of TextTest, (without the GUI), is easy to install on most platforms, and although it has fewer features, should be sufficient to give you an idea of how the approach works with this Kata.

Kata variant #4: Greenfield Gilded Rose

Imagine that the legacy system doesn't exist, and that this is instead greenfield development of the same functionality, including Conjured items. Appoint someone "Customer" and have them be the source of information about what's needed. This "Customer" could be someone who's previously done the original version of the kata and understands what the code is supposed to do. They can privately refer to the requirements document and the existing legacy code, but shouldn't show them to anyone working on the greenfield version.

---

[42]http://texttest.org

You'll be able to practice the way you gather requirements from a customer, and verify with them that you've built the right thing.

Discussion points about Designing Test Cases

- Did you need to do some refactoring before you could get the code under test at all?
- Did you make mistakes while refactoring that the tests caught?
- Have you tried running the text-based tests to see if they catch refactoring mistakes your tests have missed?
- Did you find any bugs in the code when writing your tests?
- Did you find any omissions or ambiguities in the requirements document?
- Did you miss important tests that you had to add later? Did you go back and run them against the original version of the code?
- How good is the statement coverage of your tests?
- Could you easily identify the cause of failing tests?

Discussion points about Design and Refactoring

- Were you prepared to argue with the goblin about changing the Item class? How did that decision change your design options?
- When you were refactoring, did you keep in mind the new feature you intended to add?

- Think about the design you ended up for the code. How easy would it be to add other new features? (For example weekly reports on overall stock quality, or support for interactive stocktaking)
- Review your refactoring session in a test run logging tool, (if you used one - see Tools for the Dojo). How large steps did you take? Could you have taken smaller steps?
- Were your test cases good enough to support refactoring or were you worried they missed things?

Discussion points about Variant #4: Greenfield Gilded Rose

- Is the Customer satisfied with the new system?
- Could you deploy your system now and have the Customer start using it today?
- Are you confident your code is well tested and extendable?
- Did you follow a process like Acceptance Test Driven Development or Specification By Example? Did it work well?

Ideas for after the Dojo

If you search around the internet you should be able to find plenty of blog posts about this Kata, and sample solutions. I recommend this screencast[43] of Bobby Johnson tackling the original version of this Kata. You could review his test cases[44] and compare them to the ones you've been working on.

---

[43]http://vimeo.com/34091297

[44]https://github.com/NotMyself/GildedRose/blob/first_refactor/src/GildedRose.Tests/UpdateItemsTests.cs

Contexts to use this Kata

This is a good Kata for practicing your refactoring skills, and a number of other things too. You could repeat it at several dojo meetings, trying out different variants.

Kata: Leap Years

Write a function that returns true or false depending on whether its input integer is a leap year or not.

A leap year is defined as one that is divisible by 4, but is not otherwise divisible by 100 unless it is also divisible by 400.

For example, 2001 is a typical common year and 1996 is a typical leap year, whereas 1900 is an atypical common year and 2000 is an atypical leap year.

Contexts to use this Kata

This is a very short, simple kata, it probably won't take a whole dojo meeting to do. It's a useful one for giving an introductory demonstration of TDD, since you can do it as a prepared kata in about 10-15 minutes. For complete beginners, it can help to go through the basic red-green-refactor steps in a worked example before you ask them to do it for themselves. Follow it up by getting the group to do another simple kata in a Randori form. I'd suggest FizzBuzz, Prime Factors or Tennis.

Kata: Medicine Clash

As a Health Insurer,

I want to be able to search for patients who have a medicine clash,

So that I can alert their doctors and get their prescriptions changed.

Health Insurance companies don't always get such good press, but in this case, they actually do have your best interests at heart. Some medicines interact in unfortunate ways when they get into your body at the same time, and your doctor isn't always alert enough to spot the clash when writing your prescriptions. Sometimes, medicine interactions are only identified years after the medicines become widely used, and your doctor might not be completely up to date. Your Health Insurer certainly wants you to stay healthy, so discovering a customer has a medicine clash and getting it corrected is good for business, and good for you!

For this Kata, you have a recently discovered medicine clash, and you want to look through a database of patient medicine and prescription records, to find any patients who need to be alerted to the problem. Create a "Patient" class, with a method "Clash" that takes as arguments a list of medicines, and how many days before today to consider, (defaults to the last 90 days). It should return a collection of days on which all the medicines were being taken during this time.

Data Format

You can assume the data is in a database, which is accessed in the code via an object oriented domain model. The domain model is large and complex, but for this problem you can ignore all but the following entities and attributes:

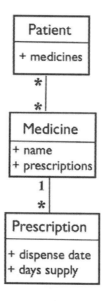

Entities and attributes for the Medicine Clash Kata

In words, this shows that each Patient has a list of Medicines. Medicines have a unique name. Each Medicine has a list of Prescriptions. Each Prescription has a dispense date and a number of days supply.

You can assume:

- patients start taking the medicine on the dispense date.

- the "days supply" tells you how many days they continue to take the medicine after the dispense date.
- if they have two overlapping prescriptions for the same medicine, they stop taking the earlier one. Imagine they have mislaid the medicine they got from the first prescription when they start on the second prescription.

There is starting skeleton code available on my github page[45].

The biology of medicine clashes[a]

When you take a pill of medicine, the active substance will be absorbed through the lining of the gut, and enter your bloodstream. That means it will be taken all over your body, and can do its work. For example, if you take a headache pill, the active substance in the drug will be taken with your blood to where it can block your pain receptors. At the same time, there are enzymes at work in your liver, which break down medicinal substances they find in your bloodstream. Eventually all the medicine will be removed, so you have to take another pill if you want the effects to continue.

In the liver, there are several different enzymes working, and they are specialized in breaking down different substances. For example, the "CYP 2C9" enzyme will break down ibuprofen, the active ingredient in many headache pills. The trouble is, there are other medicines which will stop particular enzymes from doing their work, which can lead to an overdose or other ill effects.

One example is the clash between fluoxetine and

codeine. Fluoxetine is known by its trade name "Prozac", and is often taken for depression. Codeine is another ingredient in headache pills, and is actually a "pro-drug", so it works slightly differently. Codeine needs to be broken down in the liver by the enzyme "CYP 2D6" into the active substance, morphine, before it will do anything. Fluoxetine has the effect of blocking "CYP 2D6", so if you take the two medicines together, you won't get much painkilling effect from the codeine. That could be depressing!

The solution to the problem is to take a different painkiller - one that's not affected by that liver enzyme. Simply switch codeine for ibuprofen, and you should be a little happier!

---

[a]With thanks to Sara Sjöberg for helping me to write this section

Additional discussion points for the Retrospective

- How did you handle the fact that the code relies on the current date? Did you use a mock or a stub?
- Did you learn how to use your date library better when you were doing this kata?
- How did you plan the test cases for this kata? Did you try to be comprehensive for all conceivable kinds of date overlap relative to the current date and the interesting period?
- Have you used set operations like "intersection" and "union" in your code? If not, would doing so make your code more readable?

Ideas for after the Dojo

When you've had a go at the problem yourself, and think you have a good solution for it, you might be interested to review the sample solution on my github page[46], with the same code translated into Python and Ruby. Read the code and tests and think about:

- Can you explain the algorithm that has been chosen to solve the problem?
- How readable are the tests? Do you understand what is being tested?

I find this sample code fascinating. It follows clean code guidelines with well named, short methods, and has lots of unit tests. I also find it very hard to understand. What do you think?

Another thing you could do is write some code that draws a graph visualizing when patients have taken each medicine. Something like this:

---

[46]https://github.com/emilybache/KataMedicineClash

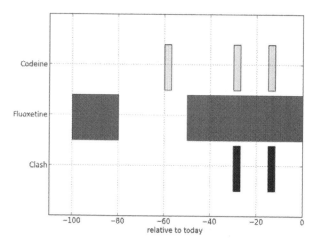

Sample Medicine Clash Visualization

Does this kind of visualization help you to identify all the edge cases you need to cover in your tests?

Contexts to use this Kata

This is a good Kata for learning about how to test code that depends on the current date, and for practicing using dates generally. I think it also lends itself to a London School style of TDD. This is a good Kata for building up an algorithm gradually, and ensuring you have tests for all the important edge cases. It also lets you think about what the best place for each test is - as a test for the Patient, Medicine or Prescription class.

Kata: Minesweeper [47]

Have you ever played Minesweeper? It's a cute little game which comes within a certain Operating System whose name we can't really remember. Well, the goal of the game is to find all the mines within an MxN field. To help you, the game shows a number in a square which tells you how many mines there are adjacent to that square. For instance, take the following 4x4 field with 2 mines (which are represented by an * character):

```
*  .  .  .
.  .  .  .
.  *  .  .
.  .  .  .
```

The same field including the hint numbers described above would look like this:

```
*  1  0  0
2  2  1  0
1  *  1  0
1  1  1  0
```

You should write a program that takes input as follows: The input will consist of an arbitrary number of fields. The

[47]This Kata was originally published by the University of Brazil as part of an international contest. http://acm.uva.es/p/v101/10189.html.

first line of each field contains two integers n and m (0 < n,m <= 100) which stands for the number of lines and columns of the field respectively. The next n lines contains exactly m characters and represent the field. Each safe square is represented by an "." character (without the quotes) and each mine square is represented by an "*" character (also without the quotes). The first field line where n = m = 0 represents the end of input and should not be processed.

Your program should produce output as follows: For each field, you must print the following message in a line alone:

```
Field #x:
```

Where x stands for the number of the field (starting from 1). The next n lines should contain the field with the "." characters replaced by the number of adjacent mines to that square. There must be an empty line between field outputs.

This is the acceptance test input:

```
4 4
*...
....
.*..
....
3 5
**...
.....
.*...
0 0
```

and output:

```
Field #1:
* 1 0 0
2 2 1 0
1 * 1 0
1 1 1 0

Field #2:
* * 1 0 0
3 3 2 0 0
1 * 1 0 0
```

Additional discussion points for the Retrospective

- What order did you implement test cases in? Was this the best order?
- Does your solution cover all the important edge cases? Really, I do mean *edge* cases!
- What datastructure did you choose to store the minefield in? Would another datastructure be more convenient? What are the tradeoffs? Would a different choice affect which test cases you should write?

Ideas for after the Dojo

Implement KataMinesweeper again using a different datastructure to store the minefield in. Alternatively, try the Kata Game of Life with the same datastructure as you used in Minesweeper.

Kata: Monty Hall

This eponymous gameshow host tempts contestants with a big prize, hidden behind one of three doors. The contestant begins by choosing a door, but not opening it. Then Monty steps forward and opens one of the other doors. He reveals a goat (!). Then the contestant has the choice of either sticking with the door they have already chosen, or switching to the other unopened door. Whichever door the contestant decides on will be opened, and if they find the prize, they get to keep it. (I'm not sure what happens if they get the second goat!) So what's the best strategy?

The Monty Hall Dilemma

That's the classic "Monty Hall Dilemma". Should you keep to your original choice of door? You could try playing the game yourself using this online version[48]?[49]

People are biased towards sticking with what they've chosen, and the vast majority of people keep the door they originally picked. Intuitively there should be an equal chance of the prize being behind any of the three doors, so it shouldn't matter if you stick or switch. However, in this case, your intuition is wrong. You are twice as likely to win the prize if you switch to the other unopened door.

---

[48]http://redsquirrel.com/dave/play/montyOnAjax.html

[49]This version was designed & built by Dave Hoover. Additional benefit: you don't run the risk of winning an actual goat.

I was not the only one to disbelieve this result, apparently even famous mathematicians have refused to accept it. What finally convinced them, was a computer simulation. So, your task is to write that computer simulation. Prove that switching doors is best, by simulating 1000 games using each strategy and comparing the winning percentage.

Additional discussion points for the Retrospective

- How did you set up your "guiding test" at the start? Did the interface you designed turn out to be a good one?
- How did you allow the tests to control the randomness of which door would have the prize?
- Did you use any mocks or stubs?
- How easily would your code cope if the number of doors were increased?

Ideas for after the Dojo

- Read this essay[50] by Martin Fowler about mocks and stubs and see if you can do this kata using either style of TDD.

Contexts to use this Kata

This kata is a little bit challenging to break down into test cases you can implement in small steps. You also have to understand how to isolate the random elements and make the code testable. Before you do the kata in your dojo, you might

---

[50]http://martinfowler.com/articles/mocksArentStubs.html

want to go through the theory of the difference between mocks and stubs. You might find it easier to do this kata with a mockist approach (London School) than a classic approach.

Kata: Phone Numbers

Given a list of phone numbers, determine if it is consistent. In a consistent phone list no number is a prefix of another. For example:

- Bob: 91 12 54 26
- Alice: 97 625 992
- Emergency: 911

In this case, it is not possible to call Bob because the phone exchange would direct your call to the emergency line as soon as you dialled the first three digits of Bob's phone number. So this list would not be consistent.

Note there are some sample phonebook datasets available on github[51].

Additional discussion points for the Retrospective

- have you written functionality to look up someone's phone number from their name?
- will your code still work if you change the order of the entries in the list?

---

[51]https://github.com/emilybache/Phone-Numbers-Kata

Ideas for after the Dojo

Can you do this kata in a functional style, without using
any loops? Look at the algorithm you've chosen. How will
it perform as the size of the phone book increases? Can you
come up with a more efficient algorithm?

Contexts to use this Kata

This is a short, straightforward kata, useful as a warm up or
demo. Similar to FizzBuzz.

Kata: Poker Hands

Compare two Poker Hands and decide which wins. A Poker hand comprises 5 cards dealt from a normal 52 card deck, and each card has a suit and a value. All suits have the same rank, for example the Ace of Clubs is not beaten by the Ace of Spades, they are equal.

A poker hand can be represented using symbols like this:

2H 3D 5S 9C KD

(Two of Hearts, 3 of Diamonds, 5 of Spades, 9 of Clubs, King of Diamonds)

The suit of the card is represented by one character:

Clubs	Diamonds	Hearts	Spades
C	D	H	S

The face value of the card is represented by another character, either the number on the face, or one of the following special cases:

10	Jack	Queen	King	Ace
T	J	Q	K	A

You compare Poker hands by deciding which has the higher rank, according to the categories below. These categories are listed in order of ascending rank. For example, a hand containing a Full House has higher rank than a hand containing a Pair.

- **High Card**: The value of the highest card in the hand. If the highest cards have the same value, the hands are ranked by the next highest, and so on.
- **Pair**: 2 of the 5 cards in the hand have the same value. Hands which both contain a pair are ranked by the value of the cards forming the pair. If these values are the same, the hands are ranked by the values of the cards not forming the pair, in decreasing order.
- **Two Pairs**: The hand contains 2 different pairs. Hands which both contain 2 pairs are ranked by the value of their highest pair. Hands with the same highest pair are ranked by the value of their other pair. If these values are the same the hands are ranked by the value of the remaining card.
- **Three of a Kind**: Three of the cards in the hand have the same value. Hands which both contain three of a kind are ranked by the value of the 3 cards.
- **Straight**: Hand contains 5 cards with consecutive values. Hands which both contain a straight are ranked by their highest card.
- **Flush**: Hand contains 5 cards of the same suit. Hands which are both flushes are ranked using the rules for High Card.
- **Full House**: 3 cards of the same value, with the remaining 2 cards forming a pair. Ranked by the value of the 3 cards.
- **Four of a kind**: 4 cards with the same value. Ranked by the value of the 4 cards.

- **Straight flush**: 5 cards of the same suit with consecutive values. Ranked by the highest card in the hand.

If you like, you can read the two hands to be compared from standard input, and write which won to standard output:

```
2H 3D 5S 9C KD 2C 3H 4S 8C AH
Player 2 wins.
```

Additional discussion points for the Retrospective

- how did you choose the order of test cases to implement?
- are all your tests for whole hands? Or do you have tests for comparing smaller numbers of cards?

Ideas for after the Dojo

Try this Kata in the London School style of TDD, (or the classic style if you already did it like that).

Contexts to use this Kata

This Kata is similar to Yatzy, but harder.

Kata: Potter[52]

Once upon a time there was a series of 5 books about a very English hero called Harry. (At least when this Kata was invented, there were only 5. Since then they have multiplied) Children all over the world thought he was fantastic, and, of course, so did the publisher. So in a gesture of immense generosity to mankind, (and to increase sales) they set up the following pricing model to take advantage of Harry's magical powers.

One copy of any of the five books costs 8 EUR. If, however, you buy two different books from the series, you get a 5% discount on those two books. If you buy 3 different books, you get a 10% discount. With 4 different books, you get a 20% discount. If you go the whole hog, and buy all 5, you get a huge 25% discount.

Note that if you buy, say, four books, of which 3 are different titles, you get a 10% discount on the 3 that form part of a set, but the fourth book still costs 8 EUR.

Potter mania is sweeping the country and parents of teenagers everywhere are queueing up with shopping baskets overflowing with Potter books. Your mission is to write a piece of code to calculate the price of any conceivable shopping basket, giving as big a discount as possible.

For example, how much does this basket of books cost?

---

[52]With thanks to Emmanuel Gaillot, who designed this Kata, for permission to include it here. See also http://xp-france.net/cgi-bin/wiki.pl?KataPotter

- 2 copies of the first book
- 2 copies of the second book
- 2 copies of the third book
- 1 copy of the fourth book
- 1 copy of the fifth book

answer: 51.20 EUR

Test Cases

These test cases are written in Ruby, but you can translate them into whatever language and tool you are using.

```
def testBasics
  assert_equal(0, price([]))
  assert_equal(8, price([0]))
  assert_equal(8, price([1]))
  assert_equal(8, price([2]))
  assert_equal(8, price([3]))
  assert_equal(8, price([4]))
  assert_equal(8 * 2, price([0, 0]))
  assert_equal(8 * 3, price([1, 1, 1]))
end

def testSimpleDiscounts
  assert_equal(8 * 2 * 0.95,
      price([0, 1]))
  assert_equal(8 * 3 * 0.9,
      price([0, 2, 4]))
  assert_equal(8 * 4 * 0.8,
      price([0, 1, 2, 4]))
```

```
    assert_equal(8 * 5 * 0.75,
        price([0, 1, 2, 3, 4]))
end

def testSeveralDiscounts
  assert_equal(8 + (8 * 2 * 0.95),
      price([0, 0, 1]))
  assert_equal(2 * (8 * 2 * 0.95),
      price([0, 0, 1, 1]))
  assert_equal((8 * 4 * 0.8) +
               (8 * 2 * 0.95),
      price([0, 0, 1, 2, 2, 3]))
  assert_equal(8 + (8 * 5 * 0.75),
      price([0, 1, 1, 2, 3, 4]))
end

def testEdgeCases
  assert_equal(2 * (8 * 4 * 0.8),
      price([0, 0, 1, 1, 2, 2, 3, 4]))
  assert_equal(3 * (8 * 5 * 0.75) +
               2 * (8 * 4 * 0.8),
      price([0, 0, 0, 0, 0,
             1, 1, 1, 1, 1,
             2, 2, 2, 2,
             3, 3, 3, 3, 3,
             4, 4, 4, 4]))
end
```

Additional discussion points for the Retrospective

- did you manage to build up the algorithm gradually, driving development with tests?
- how much work would it be to update your code if they introduced a 6th book into the series, or changed the discount percentages?

Ideas for after the Dojo

Since this is quite a big kata, you probably won't finish it in one meeting. You may want to hack at it some more by yourself. Alternatively you could write some code to come up with different book sets and discounts, and find other examples with a similar pricing quirk to this one. Another thing to do would be to research general-purpose optimization algorithms.

Contexts to use this Kata

You'll find that this Kata is easy at the start. You can get going with tests for baskets of 0 books, 1 book, 2 identical books, 2 different books... and it is not too difficult to work in small steps and gradually introduce complexity. The twist becomes apparent when you sit down and work out how much you think the sample basket above should cost. It isn't 5 * 8 * 0.75 + 3 * 8 * 0.90. It is in fact 4 * 8 * 0.8 + 4 * 8 * 0.8. So the trick with this Kata is not that the acceptance test you've been given is wrong. The trick is that you have to write some code that handles the fact that two sets of four books is cheaper than a set of five and a set of three.

It's actually very hard to write a general solution to this problem that will cope with any number of books in a set, and any conceivable discounts. Doing this kata can generate good discussions about "Do the simplest thing that could possibly work" and premature generalization. It's also quite a difficult/long kata, and you'll probably need more than one meeting before you get a working solution to this problem.

Kata: Prime Factors

Factorize a positive integer number into its prime factors.
For example:

```
 2 -> [2]
 3 -> [3]
 4 -> [2,2]
 6 -> [2,3]
 9 -> [3,3]
12 -> [2,2,3]
15 -> [3,5]
```

Additional discussion points for the Retrospective

- did you manage to build up the algorithm gradually, using TDD?
- have you thought at all about performance? What happens if you enter a really big positive integer like $2**32$?

Ideas for after the Dojo

Have a look around the internet. Lots of people have posted solutions, articles and screencasts for this kata. I'd recommend you look at Robert C. Martin's article "The Prime Factors Kata"[53], and also this article by Andrew Dalke, "Problems

---

[53]http://butunclebob.com/ArticleS.UncleBob.ThePrimeFactorsKata

with TDD"[54] which, amongst other things, criticizes Robert C. Martin's solution to this kata.

Contexts to use this Kata

This kata is similar to Roman Numerals and Bowling Game.

---

[54]http://www.dalkescientific.com/writings/diary/archive/2009/12/29/problems_with_tdd.html

Four Katas on a Racing-Car Theme

Imagine you have just started a new job working on the software systems for a Formula 1 racing team. You have inherited some code that you would characterize as legacy, and you now want to write unit tests for it. Much of the code fails to follow one or more of the SOLID principles, and this makes it more difficult.

Clone the repository on github[55], to find starting code for these four Katas that form a set. The starting code is available in a variety of programming languages, including C#, Java, Javascript and Python. Note that these katas were originally designed by Luca Minudel and published here on github[56] as part of his research into TDD and Design Principles. Also note - he really has worked for a Formula 1 racing team!

It's rather ambitious to do all four exercises in one dojo meeting. I suggest doing them over two or three meetings. I've listed the exercises here in the order you could do them in.

Instructions for all four exercises

For each exercise, there is only one class you are interested in writing tests for right now. As a first step, try to get some kind

---

[55]https://github.com/emilybache/Racing-Car-Katas
[56]https://github.com/lucaminudel/TDDwithMockObjectsAndDesignPrinciples

of test in place before you change the class at all. Identify why the class is hard to write tests for, and which SOLID principles are not being followed.

When you have some kind of test to lean on, refactor the code and make it testable. Take care when refactoring not to alter the functionality, or change interfaces which other client code may rely on. When you've refactored enough that the functionality is testable, add more tests, and continue to refactor as necessary.

Kata: Tyre Pressure Monitor[57]

The code for this Kata is in the folder called "**TirePressure-MonitoringSystem**".

The Alarm class is designed to monitor tyre pressure and set an alarm if the pressure falls outside of the expected range. The Sensor class provided for the exercise fakes the behaviour of a real tyre sensor from a racing car, providing random but realistic values.

- Write the unit tests for the **Alarm** class

Kata: Unicode File to HTML Text Converter

The code for this Kata is in the folder called "**UnicodeFileTo-HtmTextConverter**".

The UnicodeFileToHtmlTextConverter class is designed to reformat a plain text file for display in a browser.

---

[57]The American spelling of "Tyre" is "Tire".

- Write the unit tests for the **UnicodeFileToHtmlTextConverter** class.

Kata: Turn Ticket Dispenser

The code for this Kata is in the folder called "**TurnTicketDispenser**".

The TicketDispenser class is designed to be used to manage a queuing system in a shop. There may be more than one ticket dispenser but the same ticket should not be issued to two different customers.

- Write the unit tests for the **TicketDispenser** class.

Kata: Racing Car Telemetry

The code for this Kata is in the folder called "**TelemetrySystem**".

The responsibility of the TelemetryDiagnosticControls class is to establish a connection to the telemetry server (through the TelemetryClient), send a diagnostic request and successfully receive the response that contains the diagnostic info. The TelemetryClient class provided for the exercise fakes the behavior of the real TelemetryClient class, and can respond with either the diagnostic information or a random sequence. The real TelemetryClient class would connect and communicate with the telemetry server via tcp/ip, and receive information from the racing car.

- Write the unit tests for the **TelemetryDiagnosticControls** class.

Additional discussion points for the Retrospective

- What SOLID principle(s) did this code violate before you started? Does it still violate any?
- Were there any other problems with this code that are not to do with SOLID violations? Did your testing approach lead you to find them, or did you notice them some other way?
- Does using TDD ensure your code will follow SOLID principles?
- Is it possible to write code that follows the SOLID principles but is still difficult to understand and maintain?
- Is it easier or harder to follow SOLID principles in a dynamically typed language? (if you've tried this exercise in more than one language)

Ideas for after the Dojo

Re-read the descriptions of Robert C. Martin's SOLID principles and try to find violations of them in the production code you're working on. If you found other problems in the Kata code that aren't to do with SOLID violations, look for them too. How has your testing approach allowed these problems to be there? Should you change your testing approach?

Following up Kata: Turn Ticket Dispenser

You might be interested to have a look at "Working Effectively with Legacy Code" by Michael Feathers, and review the following sections:

- page 369: Introduce Instance Delegator
- page 372: Introduce Static Setter
- page 399: Replace Global Reference with Getter
- page 339: Encapsulate Global References

The descriptions there are about statically typed languages like Java and C++. The mechanics may be different in languages like Javascript or Python, but I think it's still good to understand the purpose of these refactorings.

Following up Kata: Unicode File to HTML Text Converter

You might be interested to have a look at "Working Effectively with Legacy Code" by Michael Feathers, and review the sections on "Skin and Wrap the API", and "Responsibility-Based Extraction" on page 205.

Contexts to use this Kata

Before you do these katas in your dojo, you will want to remind people of the SOLID principles, to put the katas in context. For an explanation of SOLID see wikipedia[58], or the book "Agile Software Development: Principles, Patterns, and Practices" by Robert C. Martin.

All these Katas are interesting to do with a London School approach to TDD. Luca's original study was looking at whether this leads to better adherence to SOLID principles than using classic TDD. In one of the exercises, "Tyre Pressure Monitor",

---

[58]http://en.wikipedia.org/wiki/SOLID_%28object-oriented_design%29

there is some test code provided - a hand-made Mock and Stub implementation for the Alarm interface. This code is not needed to complete the exercises, it's just there to help you to understand what a Mock and a Stub are. You could go through this code at the start of the dojo, to help people just beginning to learn the London School of TDD.

Kata: Reversi

Reversi is a board game for two players, using a 8x8 two-dimensional grid of square cells. The players take it in turns to place a disc showing their colour into a square, and take control of one or more of the discs showing the opponent's colour. The game ends when either all 64 squares are filled with a disc, or there are no legal positions for either player to place a disc. The winner is the player with the most discs showing their colour on the board.

A position is legal if it allows you to flip over one or more of the opponent's discs, ie change them to your colour. For this to happen you must place the new disc in a position where there is at least one straight (horizontal, vertical, or diagonal) occupied line between the new disc and another disc of your colour, with one or more contiguous pieces of the opponent's colour between them. For example if we have a board like this:

```
.  .  .  .  .  .  .  .
.  .  .  .  .  .  .  .
.  .  .  .  .  .  .  .
.  .  .  W  B  .  .  .
.  .  .  B  W  .  .  .
.  .  .  .  .  .  .  .
.  .  .  .  .  .  .  .
.  .  .  .  .  .  .  .
```

(where "." indicates an empty square, "B" indicates a black disc, and "W" a white disc)

there are legal moves for Black in the squares marked with a *:

```
.  .  .  .  .  .  .  .
.  .  .  .  .  .  .  .
.  .  .  *  .  .  .  .
.  .  *  W  B  .  .  .
.  .  .  B  W  *  .  .
.  .  .  .  *  .  .  .
.  .  .  .  .  .  .  .
.  .  .  .  .  .  .  .
```

Note there is more detailed information about the rules on Wikipedia[59].

For this Code Kata, you write a program that takes an arbitrary position and whose turn it is, and find all the legal positions where they could play. You don't have to use ASCII art in your code, you could output the legal positions as co-ordinates, (columns labelled A - H, rows labelled 1 - 8 starting from top left hand corner), like this: [C4, D3, E6, F5]. Alternatively come up with a better graphical visualization of the position.

Additional discussion points for the Retrospective

- Did you find a good datastructure to represent the two-dimensional orthogonal grid in your code?

---

[59]http://en.wikipedia.org/wiki/Reversi

- Did you design test cases that were small enough to get you started, yet were still passing at the end of the Kata?
- Would your code still work if the size or shape of the board changed?

Ideas for after the Dojo

If you used an object oriented language, try it again in a functional language, and vice versa.

Contexts to use this Kata

There are other katas that use a two dimensional grid, you might find it interesting to compare this one with Minesweeper and Game of Life.

Kata: Roman Numerals

The Romans were a clever bunch. They conquered most of Europe and ruled it for hundreds of years. They invented concrete and straight roads and even bikinis[60]. One thing they never discovered though was the number zero. This made writing and dating extensive histories of their exploits slightly more challenging, but the system of numbers they came up with is still in use today. For example the BBC uses Roman numerals to date their programmes.

For this Kata, write a function to convert from normal (Arabic) numbers to Roman Numerals:

```
 1 -> I
10 -> X
 7 -> VII
```

etc.

There is no need to be able to convert numbers larger than about 3000. (The Romans themselves didn't tend to go any higher).

Background information

---

[60]Check out the beautiful mosaics at the Roman Villa of Piazza Armerina

Symbol	Value
I	1
V	5
X	10
L	50
C	100
D	500
M	1000

Generally, symbols are placed in order of value, starting with the largest values. When smaller values precede larger values, the smaller values are subtracted from the larger values, and the result is added to the total. However, you can't write numerals like "IM" for 999, there are some additional rules:

- A number written in Arabic numerals can be broken into digits. For example, 1903 is composed of 1 (one thousand), 9 (nine hundreds), 0 (zero tens), and 3 (three units). To write the Roman numeral, each of the non-zero digits should be treated separately. In the above example, 1,000 = M, 900 = CM, and 3 = III. Therefore, 1903 = MCMIII.
- The symbols "I", "X", "C", and "M" can be repeated three times in succession, but no more. (They may appear more than three times if they appear non-sequentially, such as XXXIX.) "D", "L", and "V" can never be repeated.
- "I" can be subtracted from "V" and "X" only. "X" can be subtracted from "L" and "C" only. "C" can be subtracted from "D" and "M" only. "V", "L", and "D" can never be subtracted.
- Only one small-value symbol may be subtracted from any large-value symbol.

Part II

Write a function to convert in the other direction, ie numeral to digit

Additional discussion points for the Retrospective

- Did you manage to build up the algorithm gradually, driving development with tests?
- Is your choice of algorithm obvious from the code, or do you need additional comments?

Ideas for after the Dojo

You'll probably only have managed part I of the kata during the meeting, you could have a go at part II. Also have a look around the internet, lots of people have posted solutions to this kata. Review their code readability compared with yours.

Contexts to use this Kata

This is quite an easy Kata, it's a good introduction to building up an algorithm using TDD. It's quite similar to Prime Factors and Bowling Game

Kata: String Calculator[61]

Before you start

- Try not to read ahead.
- Do one task at a time. The trick is to learn to work incrementally.
- There is no need to test for invalid inputs for this kata, assume the string you receive is correctly formatted.

1. Create a simple String calculator with a method **int Add(string numbers)**
   - The method can take 0, 1 or 2 numbers, and will return their sum (for an empty string it will return 0) for example "" or "1" or "1,2"
   - Start with the simplest test case of an empty string and move to one and two numbers
   - Remember to solve things as simply as possible
   - Remember to refactor after each passing test
2. Allow the Add method to handle an unknown amount of numbers
3. Allow the Add method to handle newlines between numbers instead of commas.

---

[61]With thanks to Roy Osherove, who designed this Kata, for permission to include it here.

- The following input is valid: "1\n2,3" (will equal 6)
- The following input is **not** valid: "1,\n" (no need to handle this in your code)

4. Support different delimiters
   - To change a delimiter, the beginning of the string will contain a separate line that looks like this: "//[delimiter]\n[numbers...]" for example "//;\n1;2" should return three since the delimiter is ';' .
   - The first line is optional, so all existing scenarios should still be supported, (existing tests should still pass).

5. Calling Add with a negative number should throw an exception "negatives not allowed". The exception message should include the negative that was passed. If there are multiple negatives, list all of them in the message.

Additional discussion points for the Retrospective

- Did you ever write more code than you needed to make the current tests pass?
- Did you ever have more than one failing test at a time?
- Did the tests fail unexpectedly at any point? If so, why?
- How much did writing the tests slow you down?
- Did you write more tests than you would have if you had coded first and written tests afterwards?
- Are you happy with the design of the code you ended up with? Should you have refactored it more often?

Ideas for after the Dojo

Watch some of the example screencasts on Roy Osherove's website[62]. Many good programmers have contributed there. Is there a screencast in the language and tools you're using? How does it change the way you do TDD if you use a different programming language or toolset?

Contexts to use this Kata

This is an excellent Kata for TDD beginners. It leads you through some simple test cases and code, making you follow the rhythm of red-green-refactor. Experienced TDD:ers can profitably use it to try out new tools or languages.

[62]http://osherove.com/tdd-kata-1/

Kata: Tennis

Tennis has a rather quirky scoring system, and to newcomers it can be a little difficult to keep track of. The Tennis Society has contracted you to build a scoreboard to display the current score during tennis games. The umpire will have a handset with two buttons labelled "player 1 scores" and "player 2 scores", which he or she will press when the respective players score a point. When this happens, a big scoreboard display should update to show the current score. (When you first switch on the scoreboard, both players are assumed to have no points). When one of the players has won, the scoreboard should display which one.

Your task is to write a "TennisGame" class containing the logic which outputs the correct score as a string for display on the scoreboard. You can assume that the umpire pressing the button "player 1 scores" will result in a method "wonPoint("player1")" being called on your class, and similarly wonPoint("player2") for the other button. Afterwards, you will get a call "getScore()" from the scoreboard asking what it should display. This method should return a string with the current score. *(Note: do modify the method names to match the idiom for your programming language)*

You can read more about Tennis scores here[63] which is summarized below:

1. A game is won by the first player to have won at least four points in total and at least two points more than

[63]http://en.wikipedia.org/wiki/Tennis#Scoring

the opponent. The score is then "Win for player1" or "Win for player2"

2. The running score of each game is described in a manner peculiar to tennis: scores from zero to three points are described as "Love", "Fifteen", "Thirty", and "Forty" respectively.

3. If at least three points have been scored by each player, and the scores are equal, the score is "Deuce".

4. If at least three points have been scored by each side and a player has one more point than his opponent, the score of the game is "Advantage player1" or "Advantage player2".

The Tennis Society has agreed that Sets and Matches are out of scope, so you only need to report the score for the current game. However, they have requested another feature with lower priority. They want to be able to change the name of the players from "player1" to "Björn Borg" and "player2" to "John McEnroe". This feature has been categorized "Nice to have", or, more accurately, "in your dreams"!

Tennis Refactoring Kata

Imagine you work for a consultancy company, and one of your colleagues has been doing some work for the Tennis Society. The contract is for 10 hours billable work, and your colleague has spent 8.5 hours working on it. Unfortunately he has now fallen ill, although he says he has completed the work, and the tests all pass. Your boss has asked you to take over and spend an hour or so on it so she can bill the client for the full 10 hours. She instructs you to tidy up the code a little and perhaps make some notes so you can give your colleague some feedback on his chosen design.

There are three scenarios for this refactoring kata - imagine three different consultancy companies each with their own solution to the problem. I suggest you start with the first version of the code. When you've got that looking beautiful, start over with the second and third versions.

What is nice about this Kata is that the tests are almost exhaustive, and fast to run, so any mistakes you make while refactoring should be very obvious. You should not need to change the tests, only run them often as you refactor. The code is available on github[64], for several popular programming languages.

I also recommend that if you're doing this as a refactoring kata, that you use a tool to record your session, (see the chapter (#ToolsForTheDojo)), so you can review how large steps you took. The aim is for as small as possible, with as few refactoring mistakes as possible.

Additional discussion points for the Retrospective

- Is the code you have ended up with clean? Are there any smells?
- Are your tests exhaustive?
- Does your code express the scoring rules of Tennis in a readable manner?

---

[64]https://github.com/emilybache/Tennis-Refactoring-Kata

Refactoring version

- How did it feel to work with such fast, comprehensive tests?
- Did you make mistakes while refactoring that were caught by the tests?
- If you used a tool to record your test runs, review it. Could you have taken smaller steps?
- Did you ever make a refactoring mistake and then back out your changes? How did it feel to throw away code?
- If you never backed out any refactoring mistakes, is that because you're very skilled at refactoring?

Ideas for after the Dojo

- If you did this as a normal kata, try it as a refactoring kata (code on github[65])
- If you've done one of the three refactoring katas, try the other two. Were they easier or harder?
- Try doing all your refactoring without running the tests until you're "finished". How many tests did you break via refactoring mistakes?

Contexts to use this Kata

This is a good kata for practicing refactoring. There aren't many situations where you have the luxury of exhaustive tests. The three refactoring variants have slightly different challenges. The first two are by junior coders with poor grasp of the language. The third is designed to be as concise as possible, to the point of unreadability.

---

[65]https://github.com/emilybache/Tennis-Refactoring-Kata

Kata: Train Reservation

Railway operators aren't always known for their use of cutting edge technology, and in this case they're a little behind the times. The railway people want you to help them to improve their online booking service. They'd like to be able to not only sell tickets online, but to decide exactly which seats should be reserved, at the time of booking.

You're working on the "TicketOffice" service, and your next task is to implement the feature for reserving seats on a particular train. The railway operator has a service-oriented architecture, and both the interface you'll need to fulfill, and some services you'll need to use are already implemented.

All the starting code for this kata is available in my github repo[66]. The latest version of these instructions is also there.

Business Rules around Reservations

There are various business rules and policies around which seats may be reserved. For a train overall, no more than 70% of seats may be reserved in advance, and ideally no individual coach should have no more than 70% reserved seats either.

---

[66]https://github.com/emilybache/KataTrainReservation

However, there is another business rule that says you *must* put all the seats for one reservation in the same coach. This could make you and go over 70% for some coaches, just make sure to keep to 70% for the whole train.

The Guiding Test

The Ticket Office service needs to respond to a HTTP POST request that comes with form data telling you which train the customer wants to reserve seats on, and how many they want. It should return a json document detailing the reservation that has been made.

A reservation comprises a json document with three fields, the train id, booking reference, and the ids of the seats that have been reserved. Example json:

```
{"train_id": "express_2000",
 "booking_reference": "75bcd15",
 "seats": ["1A", "1B"]}
```

If it is not possible to find suitable seats to reserve, the service should instead return an empty list of seats and an empty string for the booking reference. The test cases in guiding_test.py outline the expected interface.

Command line option

If you think it's too hard to come up with a fully deployed HTTP service, you could instead write a command line program which takes the train id and number of seats as command line arguments, and returns the same json as above.

Booking Reference Service

You can get a unique booking reference using a REST-based service. For test purposes, you can start a local service using the provided code in the "booking_reference_service" folder. You can assume the real service will behave the same way, but be available on a different url.

Install Python 3.3[67] and CherryPy[68], then start the server by running:

```
python booking_reference_service.py
```

You can use this service to get a unique booking reference. Make a GET request to:

```
http://localhost:8082/booking_reference
```

This will return a string that looks a bit like this:

```
75bcd15
```

Train Data Service

You can get information about which each train has by using the train data service. For test purposes, you can start a local service using the provided code in the "train_data_service" folder. You can assume the real service will behave the same way, but be available on a different url.

Again, you need Python 3.3[69] and CherryPy[70], then start the server by running:

---

[67]http://python.org
[68]http://www.cherrypy.org/
[69]http://python.org
[70]http://www.cherrypy.org/

```
python start_service.py
```

You can use this service to get data for example about the train
with id "express_2000" like this:

```
http://localhost:8081/data_for_train/express_2000
```

this will return a json document with information about the
seats that this train has. The document you get back will look
for example like this:

```
{"seats": {"1A": {"booking_reference": "",
                   "seat_number": "1",
                   "coach": "A"},
           "2A": {"booking_reference": "",
                   "seat_number": "2",
                   "coach": "A"}}}
```

Note I've left out all the extraneous details about where the
train is going to and from, at what time, whether there's a
buffet car etc. All that's there is which seats the train has, and
if they are already booked. A seat is available if the "booking_-
reference" field contains an empty string. To reserve seats on
a train, you'll need to make a POST request to this url:

```
http://localhost:8081/reserve
```

and attach form data for which seats to reserve. There should
be three fields:

```
"train_id", "seats", "booking_reference"
```

The "seats" field should be a json encoded list of seat ids, for example:

```
'["1A", "2A"]'
```

The other two fields are ordinary strings. Note the server will prevent you from booking a seat that is already reserved with another booking reference.

The service has one additional method, that will remove all reservations on a particular train. Use it with care:

```
http://localhost:8081/reset/express_2000
```

Additional discussion points for the Retrospective

- Did you use the actual external services in your test or did you use a test double? What are the advantages and disadvantages?
- Does the design of your code make it easy to update the business rules about which seats can be reserved?

Ideas for after the Dojo

If you did the kata in a classic style, try it again in a London School style, and vice versa. Does it make a difference to the design you end up with?

Contexts to use this Kata

This Kata is good for practicing use of Mocks, Fakes and Stubs.

Kata: Trivia[71]

The code for this Kata is on github - you can download it from my fork[72]. It's available in a large number of programming languages, and is designed to be a Legacy Code Refactoring Kata. In order to better simulate Legacy Code, it comes with no documentation or tests.

How to use this Kata

J. B. Rainsberger uses this Kata for his "Legacy Code Retreat" events, which are a whole day, so there is enough to do in this Kata for several dojo meetings. The first thing to do is to get some test coverage in place, since if you refactor without it, you won't necessarily notice if you make a mistake and break the functionality of the code. Once you have some tests to lean on, you can practice refactoring techniques.

Add unit tests without changing any of the code

This should be quite difficult. You will learn about what makes code hard to unit test. You'll probably end up with tests that are not really "unit" tests since they test larger chunks of code.

---

[71]With thanks to Chet Hendrickson, who designed this code, for permission to use it, and also J.B. Rainsberger, who brought this Kata to my attention.

[72]https://github.com/emilybache/trivia

You could try the technique "subclass to test", in order to get the "Game" class under test.

Think about what changes you feel comfortable making to the code with the tests you've written. Measure the statement and branch coverage you get from your tests.

Add text-based tests without changing any of the code

This should be relatively straightforward. You will need to add a "seed" to control the randomness, and record output from many different games - enough to give good coverage of the functionality. I have made a video[73] about how you could do this with TextTest[74], or if you're working in C#, there is this video[75] by Llewellyn Falco, using his approval testing framework. See also the chapter on Approval testing.

Practicing refactoring techniques

- identify duplicated code, see if you can reduce duplication using "Extract Method"
- Extract *pure functions* (no state, no side effects) to find and remove the temporal coupling in the code
- Identify if there are responsibilities of the "Game" class that could be extracted into other classes, and practice the "Extract Class" refactoring.

---

[73]http://www.youtube.com/watch?v=RSvcrT3chg8
[74]http://texttest.org
[75]http://www.youtube.com/watch?v=lhE9DF2MvJ4

Additional discussion points for the Retrospective

- Why was this code so hard to write unit tests for?
- Have you found any bugs in the code?
- What are the pros and cons of tests that aren't unit tests, (because they test a larger piece of code)?
- Did you make mistakes when refactoring? Do you need to improve your refactoring skills?

Ideas for after the Dojo

Since this Kata is quite a long one, you'll probably find plenty still to work on after the dojo. You can keep refactoring the code for some time before it looks clean, and even longer before it looks beautiful.

Contexts to use this Kata

This is a good Kata for learning about getting legacy code under test. You'll find it a lot easier to get some basic regression tests in place with a text-based testing approach than a normal unit testing approach. That makes it a good kata for learning about text-based testing, as is Gilded Rose.

It's also a good Kata for improving your refactoring skills: taking many small, safe steps, adding up to a large scale improvement. Other refactoring katas are Tennis, and Yatzy.

Kata: Yatzy[76]

The game of Yatzy[77] is a simple dice game. Each player rolls five six-sided dice. They can re-roll some or all of the dice up to three times (including the original roll).

For example, suppose a players rolls (3,4,5,5,2). They hold (-,-,5,5,-) and re-roll (3,4,-,-,2) to get (5,1,5,5,3). They decide to hold (5,-,5,5,-) and re-roll (-,1,-,-,3). They end up with (5,6,5,5,2).

The player then places the roll in a category, such as ones, twos, fives, pair, two pairs etc (see below). If the roll is compatible with the category, the player gets a score for the roll according to the rules. If the roll is not compatible with the category, the player scores zero for the roll.

For example, suppose a player scores (5,6,5,5,2) in the fives category they would score 15 (three fives). The score for that go is then added to their total and the category cannot be used again in the remaining goes for that game. A full game consists of one go for each category. Thus, for their last go in a game, a player must choose their only remaining category.

Your task is to score a *given* roll in a *given* category. You do **not** have to program the random dice rolling. The game is **not** played by letting the computer choose the highest scoring category for a given roll.

---

[76]With thanks to Jon Jagger, who designed this Kata, for permission to include it here.
[77]http://en.wikipedia.org/wiki/Yatzy

Categories and Scoring Rules

Chance: The player scores the sum of all dice, no matter what they read. For example,

- 1,1,3,3,6 placed on "chance" scores 14 (1+1+3+3+6)
- 4,5,5,6,1 placed on "chance" scores 21 (4+5+5+6+1)

Yatzy: If all dice have the same number, the player scores 50 points. For example,

- 1,1,1,1,1 placed on "yatzy" scores 50
- 1,1,1,2,1 placed on "yatzy" scores 0

Ones, Twos, Threes, Fours, Fives, Sixes: The player scores the sum of the dice that reads one, two, three, four, five or six, respectively. For example,

- 1,1,2,4,4 placed on "fours" scores 8 (4+4)
- 2,3,2,5,1 placed on "twos" scores 4 (2+2)
- 3,3,3,4,5 placed on "ones" scores 0

Pair: The player scores the sum of the two highest matching dice. For example, when placed on "pair"

- 3,3,3,4,4 scores 8 (4+4)
- 1,1,6,2,6 scores 12 (6+6)
- 3,3,3,4,1 scores 6 (3+3)
- 3,3,3,3,1 scores 6 (3+3)

Two pairs: If there are two pairs of dice with the same number, the player scores the sum of these dice. For example, when placed on "two pairs"

- 1,1,2,3,3 scores 8 (1+1+3+3)
- 1,1,2,3,4 scores 0
- 1,1,2,2,2 scores 6 (1+1+2+2)

Three of a kind: If there are three dice with the same number, the player scores the sum of these dice. For example, when placed on "three of a kind"

- 3,3,3,4,5 scores 9 (3+3+3)
- 3,3,4,5,6 scores 0
- 3,3,3,3,1 scores 9 (3+3+3)

Four of a kind: If there are four dice with the same number, the player scores the sum of these dice. For example, when placed on "four of a kind"

- 2,2,2,2,5 scores 8 (2+2+2+2)
- 2,2,2,5,5 scores 0
- 2,2,2,2,2 scores 8 (2+2+2+2)

Small straight: When placed on "small straight", if the dice read (1,2,3,4,5), the player scores 15 (the sum of all the dice).

Large straight: When placed on "large straight", if the dice read (2,3,4,5,6), the player scores 20 (the sum of all the dice).

Full house: If the dice are two of a kind and three of a kind, the player scores the sum of all the dice. For example, when placed on "full house"

- 1,1,2,2,2 scores 8 (1+1+2+2+2)
- 2,2,3,3,4 scores 0
- 4,4,4,4,4 scores 0

Refactoring Kata

Jon Jagger has designed a refactoring version of this kata. I've taken the liberty of putting various language versions of it here on github[78], or you can do the kata directly in the Cyber-Dojo. See the article "Yahtzee Cyber-Dojo Refactoring"[79] for information about that. While you are doing this refactoring kata, note down all the code smells you see and address

Simplification & Extension

If you're short of time for this kata, one simplification is to have it always return the sum of the dice, or zero. So the implementation just has to work out if the dice match a category or not.

If you'd like to extend the exercise, try adding a requirement to take a given roll, and return a sorted list of all the categories that give a non-zero score for it. Then you're half-way to an AI that can play the game for you...

Additional discussion points for the Retrospective

- How much duplication is there in your solution? In your test code?

---

[78]https://github.com/emilybache/Yatzy-Refactoring-Kata

[79]http://jonjagger.blogspot.co.uk/2012/05/yahtzee-cyber-dojo-refactoring-in-java.html

- Did you write a list of test cases before you started? How did you decide what order to implement them in?
- If you did this as a refactoring kata, discuss the code smells you identified. Do you have them in your production code?

Ideas for after the Dojo

Do this kata again from scratch and tackle the test cases in a different order. Does this affect the design you end up with? Can you take the tests in any order at all?

If you'd like more practice at choosing test case order, try the Minesweeper Kata, or the Tennis Kata, or Greenfield Gilded Rose. Be sure to make a list of test cases before you start, and be mindful of what order you could best implement them in.

Contexts to use this Kata

This Kata is quite easy for TDD beginners since the test cases are more or less enumerated in the problem description. The order to implement them in is not prescribed, though, so you can practice that aspect of TDD.

Further Reading

If you've enjoyed this book, and are finding it useful in your Coding Dojo, you might also like to read some of these books. Many of them contain worked code examples that you could go through in the dojo, and perhaps turn into Code Katas. Some of them you'll find I already have done! In any case, they're books that you have to do more than just *read* to get the most out of. They're full of *code*, and you're a *coder*, right?

Refactoring and Design

- "Refactoring: Improving the design of existing code", Martin Fowler
- "Refactoring to Patterns", Joshua Kerievsky
- "Working Effectively with Legacy Code", Michael Feathers
- "Agile Software Development: Principles, Patterns and Practices", Robert C. Martin

TDD, Clean Code

- "Test-Driven Development by Example", Kent Beck
- "The art of Unit Testing with examples in .NET", Roy Osherove
- "Clean Code", Robert C. Martin
- "Code Complete", Steve McConnell
- "xUnit Test Patterns", Gerard Meszaros

London School of TDD

- "Growing Object Oriented Software, Guided by Tests", Steve Freeman and Nat Price
- "The RSpec book", David Chelimsky et al

Functional Programming

- "Functional Programming for the Object-Oriented Programmer", Brian Marick

Interesting Books for Coders (except with less actual code)

- "Extreme Programming Explained", Kent Beck
- "The Pragmatic Programmer", Andrew Hunt and David Thomas
- "Apprenticeship Patterns: Guidance for the Aspiring Software Craftsman", Dave Hoover, Adewale Oshineye

A sequel to this book

To expand on some of the topics in this book, I'm writing a sequel, which you might be interested in. It uses Code Katas to illustrate coding techniques:

- "Mocks, Fakes and Stubs"[80]

---

[80]https://leanpub.com/mocks-fakes-stubs

Made in the USA
Las Vegas, NV
06 October 2021